Budgeting Mastery
Journal

Volume 2 of 2

Budgeting
Made Simple.

HABIT NEST

Your home for building healthy lifestyle habits.

habitnest.com

For information about permission to reproduce elections from this book,
email **team@habitnest.com**

Visit our website at **habitnest.com**

Publishers Disclaimer

While the publisher and author have used their best efforts in preparing this book, they make no representations or warranties with respect to the accuracy or completeness of the contents of this book. The advice and strategies contained herein may not be suitable for your situation. You should consult with a professional where appropriate. Neither the publisher nor the author shall be liable for any loss of profit or any other commercial damages, including but not limited to special, incidental, consequential, or other damages. The company, product, and service names used in this book are for identification purposes only. All trademarks and registered trademarks are the property of their respective owners.

Special Thanks

We'd like to extend a wholehearted, sincere thank you to our entire Habit Nest team for all their help in bringing this project to life. We love you all! Learn more about our team at **habitnest.com/team**

We love ya!

ISBN: 9781950045181

First edition

The Habit Nest Mission

We are a team of people obsessed with taking ACTION and learning new things as quickly as possible.

We love finding the fastest, most effective ways to build a new skill, then systemizing that process for others.

With building new habits, we empathize with others every step of the way because we go through the same process ourselves. We live and breathe everything in our company.

We use our hard-earned intuition to outline beautifully designed, intuitive products to help people live happier, more fulfilled lives.

Everything we create comes with a mix of bite-sized information, strategy, and accountability. This hands you a simple yet drastically effective roadmap to build any skill or habit with.

We take this a step further by diving into published scientific studies, the opinions of subject-matter experts, and the feedback we get from customers to further enhance all the products we create.

Ultimately, Habit Nest is a practical, action-oriented startup aimed at helping others take back decisional authority over every action they take. We're here to help people live wholesome, rewarding lives at the brink of their potential!

— Amir Atighehchi, Ari Banayan, & Mikey Ahdoot. Cofounders of Habit Nest

Contents

Our Mission in Creating This Journal

While you might already be familiar with budgeting by now, learning never ends. Over time, you will continue to to refine your budget and grow a wealth of knowledge about your finances.

With most journals, you're on your own after you run out of pages. At Habit Nest, we strive to help you through each stage of your personal development journey by continuing to offer you resources and valuable insights long after you finish your journal and solidify your new, awesome habit.

We want to help hold you accountable and continue to provide you with every necessary resource so you can continue to stay consistent with your budgeting goals. We formulate these journals with your individual needs in mind. Our role in your journey is not a role that we take lightly, and we are honored to be part of it.

Life-altering changes take time, learning, and continuous action. The main goal of this sidekick journal is to:

1. Sharpen and refine the skills you learned in the previous journal.
2. Offer you more support and resources for learning about budgeting and personal finances.
3. Continue to work towards developing your budgeting habits and get them as ingrained in your system as possible.
4. Keep you on-track and accountable.

The fact that you even cracked open this journal is a powerful sign of your dedication to bettering yourself and reaching your goals. It's an empowering feeling to take charge of your future and have everything you need right in front of you without the daunting task of sifting through resources.

By continuing to practice the concepts from the first *Budgeting Sidekick Journal*, you are better able to remain actionable, motivated, intentional, and ever-growing toward your goal of bettering yourself!

Celebrate Your Progress and the Path Ahead

Congratulations on making it to Volume 2 of the *Budgeting Sidekick Journal*!

This should mean that you conquered your first *Budgeting Sidekick Journal* and wanted to keep pushing ahead. Hopefully you're already seeing the impact on your life and your habits.

The fact that you're holding this journal and reading it speaks volumes about your character and determination! It proves how serious and committed you are to bettering yourself and making amazing changes. Your progress is something to be monumentally proud of!

Even if you stumbled a bit in the process of completing Volume 1, you pulled yourself back up. You dusted yourself off and you continued forging your path. That's no easy feat, but *you did it!*

There's no limit to how far the journey toward your goals can take you. The value lies in the journey, in everything that you have learned and how you strengthen yourself along the way. Enjoy the view, keep your head high, and hit those goals harder than ever!

CONTEMPLATION   ACTION   ROADMAP TO BEHAVIOR CHANGE

UNAWARE   PLANNING   KEEP IT GOING

The Why

Understanding Your Why

In Volume 1, we went through the process of connecting with your 'why,' which is the absolute most important aspect of changing your life for the better.

It is wise to re-evaluate and re-connect with your 'why' as often as possible. It's likely that over time your 'why' will change, take on new meaning, newfound importance, and for that reason, we would love for you to answer the following questions again.

2

The point of this is to guide you to make concrete decisions about how to approach setting your outward financial goals, and inward experience in relation to those goals.

Seriously. Take the time to define your dream life.

1. What would your life look like if you really took full control of your finances? (Think: what is the reason you bought this journal?)

....
....
....
....
....
....

2. What do you want your financial situation to realistically look like 6 months from now when you're done with this journal?

....
....
....
....
....
....

3. How would taking this budgeting process very seriously
   help you get to your ideal financial situation?

....

....

....

....

....

4. What sort of ripple effect would doing this have on other areas
   of your life? On other people's lives around you?

....

....

....

....

....

5. What would your life look like if you do not do this? What would
   you be missing out on? How would missing those make you feel?

....

....

....

....

....

6. What life goals do you consistently avoid thinking about or making time for related to money?

....

....

....

....

....

Bonus Question: What are the top hurdles you're facing with sticking to building this new habit?

....

....

....

....

....

Bookmark this section and flip back here the next time you're struggling to stay consistent with this habit.

This section is your SOS Lifeline.

The How

Continuing the Process

This journal works in the same way that Volume 1 did. It allows you to examine, track, analyze, and organize your spending habits on a daily basis. It also asks you valuable self-reflection questions that help you ground yourself and pursue your goals.

In case you need a refresher, here's how the journal works:

Monthly Tracking:

1. Before every month, you'll estimate your household income for the month.

2. You'll 'spend' that income on paper - every dollar of it will be accounted for. This is equivalent to setting your monthly goal.

3. At the end of every month, you'll compare your predictions with what you actually ended up spending, saving, and spending towards debts.

Daily Tracking:

On a daily basis, you're going to be working with the journal to plan and execute your budget.

A part of every month's preparation will include creating your savings goal and your **'flexible spending budget.'**
The savings goal + flexible spending budget refers to the amount of money you have after you account for all fixed expenses (the expense you have no choice but to pay every month).

You'll use your flexible spending budget to create a DAILY budget based on the number of days in the month.

Every day, you'll start with your flexible spending budget for the month, and subtract all the expenses from the day.

This will help you have an exact picture of how much you can spend every day without going over-budget. Keep in mind that if you over-spend some days, you can fix the direction of the ship by taking it easy on other days, so don't get down on yourself for going above your flexible daily budget.

> If all of this looks or feels overwhelming, don't worry. It looks more complicated than it is!
>
> We're also always here to help - email us at **support@habitnest.com** if you have ANY questions.

One Simple Idea

We hope that after reading the introductory pages, you're motivated and ready to tackle tomorrow with every ounce of energy you have.

We'll leave you to it with a breakdown of one simple idea...

1

Tomorrow, you will be exactly
who you are today.

2

The rest of your life is a future
projection of who you are today.

3

If you change today,
tomorrow will be different.

4

If you don't change today,
the rest of your life is predetermined.

Commit.

This week:
No matter what happens each day...

...whether I am exhausted
*or have the **worst** day of my life...*

...whether I win the lottery
*or have the **best** day of my life...*

*I **will** stick to my budgeting plan*
for the next week.

*My word is like **gold.***

I will do whatever it takes to make this happen.

I am in charge of my financial wellbeing.

_____   _____
Signature   Date

Month 1
Days
01 - 31

Monthly Budget Preparation

My main financial goal for the month:

This Month's Forecast: <u>Income</u>

Income Category	Forecasted Amount
Total Active Income	$
Total Passive Income	$
Any Other Income	$
This Month's Forecasted Income	$

This Month's Budget: <u>Fixed Expenses</u>

Fixed Expense Category	Budget
Rent/Mortgage	$
Bills	$
Car Payments	$
Insurance	$
Subscriptions	$
Other	$
This Month's Fixed Expense Budget	$

Debt Clearing Planner

Debt Name	Total Balance Remaining	Budget	Total Month's Remaining to Complete
	$	$	
	$	$	
	$	$	
	$	$	
	$	$	
	$	$	
	$	$	
	$	$	
	$	$	
	$	$	
This Month's Debt Budget			

$ ....   — $ ....   — $ ....

(This Month's Forecasted Income)   *(This Month's Fixed Expense Budget)*   *(This Month's Debt Budget)*

= $ ....

(This Month's Remaining Balance)

1. Now, choose how to allocate this remaining balance based on your personalized goals.

Note: These two fields' totals should add up to "This Month's Remaining Balance."

$ .... $ ....

(This Month's Savings Goal)   *(This Month's Flexible Expense Budget)*

2. Next, take "This Month's Flexible Expense Budget" and break it down based on the following categories:

This Month's Budget: **Flexible Expenses**	
Flexible Expense Category	**This Month's Budget**
Groceries	$
Household Necessities	$
Self-Care/Wellness	$
Entertainment	$
Outside Food/Drink	$
Other Indulgences	$
Other Transportation	$
Other	$
This Month's Flexible Expense Budget	$

3. Lastly, we'll calculate the daily budget you need to adhere to in order to achieve your monthly budgeting goal:

$ ....   ÷   ....   = $ ....

(This Month's Flexible Expense Budget)   *(Total Days In Upcoming Month)*   *(Base Daily Budget)*

_____ , 20 _____

(Month)

(Year)

(This is an optional tool you can use to help get a visual overview of your entire month)

Mon	Tue	Wed	Thu	Fri	Sat	Sun

(At the top of the right column, fill in your "Base Daily Budget" as calculated previously. Then, subtract each line item and write the resulting total as your "Leftover Balance.").

Day 01		
Flexible Expense Name	**Category**	**Today's Daily Budget:** $ _____
		- $
		- $
		- $
		- $
		- $
		- $
		- $
		- $
	Leftover Balance	**= $**

$ .... + $ .... = $ ....

(Base Daily Budget)   *(Yesterday's Leftover Balance)*   *(Today's Daily Budget)*

Day 02		
Flexible Expense Name	**Category**	**Today's Daily Budget:** $ _____
		- $
		- $
		- $
		- $
		- $
		- $
		- $
		- $
	Leftover Balance	**= $**

$ .... + $ .... = $ ....
(Base Daily Budget)   (Yesterday's Leftover Balance)   (Today's Daily Budget)

Day 03		
Flexible Expense Name	**Category**	**Today's Daily Budget:** $ _____
		- $
		- $
		- $
		- $
		- $
		- $
		- $
		- $
	Leftover Balance	**= $**

$ .... + $ .... = $ ....
(Base Daily Budget)   (Yesterday's Leftover Balance)   (Today's Daily Budget)

Day 04		
Flexible Expense Name	**Category**	**Today's Daily Budget:** $ _____
		- $
		- $
		- $
		- $
		- $
		- $
		- $
		- $
	Leftover Balance	**= $**

$ .... + $ .... = $ ....
(Base Daily Budget)   (Yesterday's Leftover Balance)   (Today's Daily Budget)

Day 05		
Flexible Expense Name	**Category**	**Today's Daily Budget:** $ _____
		- $
		- $
		- $
		- $
		- $
		- $
		- $
	Leftover Balance	= $

$ .... + $ .... = $ ....
(Base Daily Budget)   (Yesterday's Leftover Balance)   (Today's Daily Budget)

Day 06		
Flexible Expense Name	**Category**	**Today's Daily Budget:** $ _____
		- $
		- $
		- $
		- $
		- $
		- $
		- $
		- $
	Leftover Balance	= $

$ .... + $ .... = $ ....
(Base Daily Budget)   (Yesterday's Leftover Balance)   (Today's Daily Budget)

Day 07		
Flexible Expense Name	**Category**	**Today's Daily Budget:** $ _____
		- $
		- $
		- $
		- $
		- $
		- $
		- $
		- $
	Leftover Balance	**= $**

Weekly Reconciliation	
Flexible Expense Category	**This Week's Spend**
Groceries	$
Household Necessities	$
Self-Care/Wellness	$
Entertainment	$
Outside Food/Drink	$
Other Indulgences	$
Other Transportation	$
Other	$
Total Weekly Spend	$

$ .... + $ .... = $ ....
(Base Daily Budget)   (Yesterday's Leftover Balance)   (Today's Daily Budget)

Day 08		
Flexible Expense Name	**Category**	**Today's Daily Budget:** $ _____
		- $
		- $
		- $
		- $
		- $
		- $
		- $
	Leftover Balance	**= $**

$ .... + $ .... = $ ....
(Base Daily Budget)   (Yesterday's Leftover Balance)   (Today's Daily Budget)

Day 09		
Flexible Expense Name	**Category**	**Today's Daily Budget:** $ _____
		- $
		- $
		- $
		- $
		- $
		- $
		- $
		- $
	Leftover Balance	**= $**

$ .... + $ .... = $ ....

(Base Daily Budget)   (Yesterday's Leftover Balance)   (Today's Daily Budget)

Day 10

Flexible Expense Name	Category	Today's Daily Budget: $ _____
		- $
		- $
		- $
		- $
		- $
		- $
		- $
		- $
	Leftover Balance	= $

$ .... + $ .... = $ ....

(Base Daily Budget)   (Yesterday's Leftover Balance)   (Today's Daily Budget)

Day 11

Flexible Expense Name	Category	Today's Daily Budget: $ _____
		- $
		- $
		- $
		- $
		- $
		- $
		- $
		- $
	Leftover Balance	= $

$ .... + $ .... = $ ....
(Base Daily Budget)   (Yesterday's Leftover Balance)   (Today's Daily Budget)

Day 12		
Flexible Expense Name	**Category**	**Today's Daily Budget:** $\$$ _____
		- $
		- $
		- $
		- $
		- $
		- $
		- $
		- $
	Leftover Balance	= $

$ .... + $ .... = $ ....
(Base Daily Budget)   (Yesterday's Leftover Balance)   (Today's Daily Budget)

Day 13		
Flexible Expense Name	**Category**	**Today's Daily Budget:** $\$$ _____
		- $
		- $
		- $
		- $
		- $
		- $
		- $
		- $
	Leftover Balance	= $

$ .... (Base Daily Budget)   + $ .... (Yesterday's Leftover Balance)   = $ .... (Today's Daily Budget)

Day 14		
Flexible Expense Name	**Category**	**Today's Daily Budget:** $ _____
		- $
		- $
		- $
		- $
		- $
		- $
		- $
		- $
	Leftover Balance	**= $**

Weekly Reconciliation	
Flexible Expense Category	**This Week's Spend**
Groceries	$
Household Necessities	$
Self-Care/Wellness	$
Entertainment	$
Outside Food/Drink	$
Other Indulgences	$
Other Transportation	$
Other	$
Total Weekly Spend	$

$ .... + $ .... = $ ....
(Base Daily Budget)   (Yesterday's Leftover Balance)   (Today's Daily Budget)

Day 15		
Flexible Expense Name	**Category**	**Today's Daily Budget:** $ _____
		- $
		- $
		- $
		- $
		- $
		- $
		- $
		- $
	Leftover Balance	= $

$ .... + $ .... = $ ....
(Base Daily Budget)   (Yesterday's Leftover Balance)   (Today's Daily Budget)

Day 16		
Flexible Expense Name	**Category**	**Today's Daily Budget:** $ _____
		- $
		- $
		- $
		- $
		- $
		- $
		- $
		- $
	Leftover Balance	= $

$ .... + $ .... = $ ....
(Base Daily Budget)   (Yesterday's Leftover Balance)   (Today's Daily Budget)

Day 17		
Flexible Expense Name	**Category**	**Today's Daily Budget:** $ _____
		- $
		- $
		- $
		- $
		- $
		- $
		- $
		- $
	Leftover Balance	= $

$ .... + $ .... = $ ....
(Base Daily Budget)   (Yesterday's Leftover Balance)   (Today's Daily Budget)

Day 18		
Flexible Expense Name	**Category**	**Today's Daily Budget:** $ _____
		- $
		- $
		- $
		- $
		- $
		- $
		- $
		- $
	Leftover Balance	= $

$ ....   + $ ....   = $ ....

(Base Daily Budget)   (Yesterday's Leftover Balance)   (Today's Daily Budget)

Day 19		
Flexible Expense Name	**Category**	**Today's Daily Budget:** $ _____
		– $
		– $
		– $
		– $
		– $
		– $
		– $
		– $
	Leftover Balance	= $

$ ....   + $ ....   = $ ....

(Base Daily Budget)   (Yesterday's Leftover Balance)   (Today's Daily Budget)

Day 20		
Flexible Expense Name	**Category**	**Today's Daily Budget:** $ _____
		– $
		– $
		– $
		– $
		– $
		– $
		– $
		– $
	Leftover Balance	= $

$ .... + $ .... = $ ....

Day 21		
Flexible Expense Name	**Category**	**Today's Daily Budget:** $ _____
		- $
		- $
		- $
		- $
		- $
		- $
		- $
		- $
	Leftover Balance	**= $**

Weekly Reconciliation	
Flexible Expense Category	**This Week's Spend**
Groceries	$
Household Necessities	$
Self-Care/Wellness	$
Entertainment	$
Outside Food/Drink	$
Other Indulgences	$
Other Transportation	$
Other	$
Total Weekly Spend	$

$ .... + $ .... = $ ....
(Base Daily Budget)   (Yesterday's Leftover Balance)   (Today's Daily Budget)

Day 22		
Flexible Expense Name	**Category**	**Today's Daily Budget:** $ _____
		- $
		- $
		- $
		- $
		- $
		- $
		- $
		- $
	Leftover Balance	= $

$ .... + $ .... = $ ....
(Base Daily Budget)   (Yesterday's Leftover Balance)   (Today's Daily Budget)

Day 23		
Flexible Expense Name	**Category**	**Today's Daily Budget:** $ _____
		- $
		- $
		- $
		- $
		- $
		- $
		- $
		- $
	Leftover Balance	= $

$ .... + $ .... = $ ....

(Base Daily Budget)   (Yesterday's Leftover Balance)   (Today's Daily Budget)

Day 24		
Flexible Expense Name	**Category**	**Today's Daily Budget:** $ _____
		- $
		- $
		- $
		- $
		- $
		- $
		- $
		- $
	Leftover Balance	= $

$ .... + $ .... = $ ....

(Base Daily Budget)   (Yesterday's Leftover Balance)   (Today's Daily Budget)

Day 25		
Flexible Expense Name	**Category**	**Today's Daily Budget:** $ _____
		- $
		- $
		- $
		- $
		- $
		- $
		- $
		- $
	Leftover Balance	= $

$ _____ + $ _____ = $ _____
(Base Daily Budget)   (Yesterday's Leftover Balance)   (Today's Daily Budget)

Day 26		
Flexible Expense Name	**Category**	**Today's Daily Budget:** $ _____
		- $
		- $
		- $
		- $
		- $
		- $
		- $
		- $
	Leftover Balance	= $

$ _____ + $ _____ = $ _____
(Base Daily Budget)   (Yesterday's Leftover Balance)   (Today's Daily Budget)

Day 27		
Flexible Expense Name	**Category**	**Today's Daily Budget:** $ _____
		- $
		- $
		- $
		- $
		- $
		- $
		- $
		- $
	Leftover Balance	= $

$ .... + $ .... = $ ....

(Base Daily Budget)   (Yesterday's Leftover Balance)   (Today's Daily Budget)

Day 28		
Flexible Expense Name	**Category**	**Today's Daily Budget:** $ _____
		- $
		- $
		- $
		- $
		- $
		- $
		- $
		- $
	Leftover Balance	= $

Weekly Reconciliation	
Flexible Expense Category	**This Week's Spend**
Groceries	$
Household Necessities	$
Self-Care/Wellness	$
Entertainment	$
Outside Food/Drink	$
Other Indulgences	$
Other Transportation	$
Other	$
Total Weekly Spend	$

$ .... + $ .... = $ ....
(Base Daily Budget)   (Yesterday's Leftover Balance)   (Today's Daily Budget)

Day 29		
Flexible Expense Name	**Category**	**Today's Daily Budget:** $ _____
		- $
		- $
		- $
		- $
		- $
		- $
		- $
		- $
	Leftover Balance	= $

$ .... + $ .... = $ ....
(Base Daily Budget)   (Yesterday's Leftover Balance)   (Today's Daily Budget)

Day 30		
Flexible Expense Name	**Category**	**Today's Daily Budget:** $ _____
		- $
		- $
		- $
		- $
		- $
		- $
		- $
		- $
	Leftover Balance	= $

$ .... + $ .... = $ ....
(Base Daily Budget)   (Yesterday's Leftover Balance)   (Today's Daily Budget)

Day 31		
Flexible Expense Name	**Category**	**Today's Daily Budget:** $ _____
		- $
		- $
		- $
		- $
		- $
		- $
		- $
		- $
	Leftover Balance	**= $**

Weekly Reconciliation	
Flexible Expense Category	**This Week's Spend**
Groceries	$
Household Necessities	$
Self-Care/Wellness	$
Entertainment	$
Outside Food/Drink	$
Other Indulgences	$
Other Transportation	$
Other	$
Total Weekly Spend	$

Month 1 Done.

Recapping Last Month

Monthly Reconciliation: <u>Income</u>		
Income Category	**Last Month's Forecasted Income**	**Last Month's Actual Income**
Total Active Income	$	$
Total Passive Income	$	$
Any Other Income	$	$
Total Monthly Income	$	$

(You can easily get your "Actual Amount Spent Last Month" values by summing up the "Total Weekly Spend" values in your weekly reconciliations)

Monthly Reconciliation: <u>Flexible Expenses</u>		
Flexible Expense Category	**Last Month's Budget**	**Actual Amount Spent Last Month**
Groceries	$	$
Household Necessities	$	$
Self-Care/Wellness	$	$
Entertainment	$	$
Outside Food/Drink	$	$
Other Indulgences	$	$
Other Transportation	$	$
Other	$	$
Total Monthly Flexible Expenses	$	$

Monthly Reconciliation: **Fixed Expenses**

Fixed Expense Category	Last Month's Budget	Actual Amount Spent Last Month
Rent/Mortgage	$	$
Bills	$	$
Car Payments	$	$
Insurance	$	$
Subscriptions	$	$
Other	$	$
Total Monthly Fixed Expenses	$	$

Monthly Reconciliation: **Debt Balance**

Debt Name	Beginning of Last Month Balance	Amount Budgeted For Last Month	Actual Amount Paid Last Month	Remaining Debt Balance
	$	$	$	$
	$	$	$	$
	$	$	$	$
	$	$	$	$
	$	$	$	$
	$	$	$	$
	$	$	$	$
	$	$	$	$
	$	$	$	$
	$	$	$	$
Debt Totals	$	$	$	$

Recap Questions

1. What did I overspend on unnecessarily this month?
   Why do I think that happened?

   ....

   ....

   ....

2. What adjustments do I need to make to my spending
   to set my future self up in a much better position?

   ....

   ....

   ....

3. What will I tell myself if I spend over my daily budget one day?
   What actions will I take the following day(s) to get back on track?

   ....

   ....

   ....

4. In what ways can I be more supportive and forgiving of
   myself on this journey? How am I being too hard on myself?

   ....

   ....

   ....

Month 2
Days
32 - 62

Monthly Budget Preparation

My main financial goal for the month:

This Month's Forecast: __Income__

Income Category	Forecasted Amount
Total Active Income	$
Total Passive Income	$
Any Other Income	$
This Month's Forecasted Income	$

This Month's Budget: __Fixed Expenses__

Fixed Expense Category	Budget
Rent/Mortgage	$
Bills	$
Car Payments	$
Insurance	$
Subscriptions	$
Other	$
This Month's Fixed Expense Budget	$

Debt Clearing Planner

Debt Name	Total Balance Remaining	Budget	Total Month's Remaining to Complete
	$	$	
	$	$	
	$	$	
	$	$	
	$	$	
	$	$	
	$	$	
	$	$	
	$	$	
	$	$	
This Month's Debt Budget			

$ _____   — $ _____   — $ _____

(This Month's   (This Month's   (This Month's
Forecasted Income)   Fixed Expense Budget)   Debt Budget)

= $ _____

(This Month's
Remaining Balance)

1. Now, choose how to allocate this remaining balance based on your personalized goals.

Note: These two fields' totals should add up to "This Month's Remaining Balance."

$ _____ $ _____

(This Month's   (This Month's Flexible
Savings Goal)   Expense Budget)

2. Next, take "This Month's Flexible Expense Budget" and break it down based on the following categories:

This Month's Budget: __Flexible Expenses__	
Flexible Expense Category	**This Month's Budget**
Groceries	$
Household Necessities	$
Self-Care/Wellness	$
Entertainment	$
Outside Food/Drink	$
Other Indulgences	$
Other Transportation	$
Other	$
This Month's Flexible Expense Budget	$

3. Lastly, we'll calculate the daily budget you need to adhere to in order to achieve your monthly budgeting goal:

$ _____   ÷   _____   = $ _____

(This Month's Flexible   (Total Days In   (Base Daily Budget)
Expense Budget)   Upcoming Month)

_____ , 20 ___

(This is an optional tool you can use to help get a visual overview of your entire month)

Mon	Tue	Wed	Thu	Fri	Sat	Sun

$ .... + $ .... = $ ....
(Base Daily Budget)   (Yesterday's Leftover Balance)   (Today's Daily Budget)

Day 32		
Flexible Expense Name	**Category**	**Today's Daily Budget:** $ _____
		- $
		- $
		- $
		- $
		- $
		- $
		- $
		- $
	Leftover Balance	= $

$ .... + $ .... = $ ....
(Base Daily Budget)   (Yesterday's Leftover Balance)   (Today's Daily Budget)

Day 33		
Flexible Expense Name	**Category**	**Today's Daily Budget:** $ _____
		- $
		- $
		- $
		- $
		- $
		- $
		- $
		- $
	Leftover Balance	= $

$ .... $ + $ .... $ = $ .... $

(Base Daily Budget)   (Yesterday's Leftover Balance)   (Today's Daily Budget)

Day 34		
Flexible Expense Name	**Category**	**Today's Daily Budget:** $ _____
		- $
		- $
		- $
		- $
		- $
		- $
		- $
	Leftover Balance	**= $**

$ .... $ + $ .... $ = $ .... $

(Base Daily Budget)   (Yesterday's Leftover Balance)   (Today's Daily Budget)

Day 35		
Flexible Expense Name	**Category**	**Today's Daily Budget:** $ _____
		- $
		- $
		- $
		- $
		- $
		- $
		- $
		- $
	Leftover Balance	**= $**

$ .... + $ .... = $ ....
(Base Daily Budget)   (Yesterday's Leftover Balance)   (Today's Daily Budget)

Day 36		
Flexible Expense Name	**Category**	**Today's Daily Budget:** $ _____
		- $
		- $
		- $
		- $
		- $
		- $
		- $
		- $
	Leftover Balance	= $

$ .... + $ .... = $ ....
(Base Daily Budget)   (Yesterday's Leftover Balance)   (Today's Daily Budget)

Day 37		
Flexible Expense Name	**Category**	**Today's Daily Budget:** $ _____
		- $
		- $
		- $
		- $
		- $
		- $
		- $
		- $
	Leftover Balance	= $

$ .... + $ .... = $ ....
(Base Daily Budget)   (Yesterday's Leftover Balance)   (Today's Daily Budget)

Day 38		
Flexible Expense Name	**Category**	**Today's Daily Budget:** $ _____
		- $
		- $
		- $
		- $
		- $
		- $
		- $
		- $
	Leftover Balance	= $

Weekly Reconciliation	
Flexible Expense Category	**This Week's Spend**
Groceries	$
Household Necessities	$
Self-Care/Wellness	$
Entertainment	$
Outside Food/Drink	$
Other Indulgences	$
Other Transportation	$
Other	$
Total Weekly Spend	$

$ ....   + $ ....   = $ ....

    (Base Daily Budget)   *(Yesterday's Leftover Balance)*   *(Today's Daily Budget)*

Day 39		
Flexible Expense Name	**Category**	**Today's Daily Budget:** $ _____
		- $
		- $
		- $
		- $
		- $
		- $
		- $
		- $
	Leftover Balance	**= $**

$ ....   + $ ....   = $ ....

    (Base Daily Budget)   *(Yesterday's Leftover Balance)*   *(Today's Daily Budget)*

Day 40		
Flexible Expense Name	**Category**	**Today's Daily Budget:** $ _____
		- $
		- $
		- $
		- $
		- $
		- $
		- $
		- $
	Leftover Balance	**= $**

$ .... + $ .... = $ ....
(Base Daily Budget)   *(Yesterday's Leftover Balance)*   *(Today's Daily Budget)*

Day 41		
Flexible Expense Name	**Category**	**Today's Daily Budget:** $ _____
		- $
		- $
		- $
		- $
		- $
		- $
		- $
		- $
	Leftover Balance	**= $**

$ .... + $ .... = $ ....
(Base Daily Budget)   *(Yesterday's Leftover Balance)*   *(Today's Daily Budget)*

Day 42		
Flexible Expense Name	**Category**	**Today's Daily Budget:** $ _____
		- $
		- $
		- $
		- $
		- $
		- $
		- $
		- $
	Leftover Balance	**= $**

$ .... + $ .... = $ ....

(Base Daily Budget)   (Yesterday's Leftover Balance)   (Today's Daily Budget)

Day 43		
Flexible Expense Name	**Category**	**Today's Daily Budget:** $ _____
		- $
		- $
		- $
		- $
		- $
		- $
		- $
		- $
	Leftover Balance	**= $**

$ .... + $ .... = $ ....

(Base Daily Budget)   (Yesterday's Leftover Balance)   (Today's Daily Budget)

Day 44		
Flexible Expense Name	**Category**	**Today's Daily Budget:** $ _____
		- $
		- $
		- $
		- $
		- $
		- $
		- $
		- $
	Leftover Balance	**= $**

$ _____ + $ _____ = $ _____
(Base Daily Budget)   (Yesterday's Leftover Balance)   (Today's Daily Budget)

Day 45		
Flexible Expense Name	**Category**	**Today's Daily Budget:** $ _____
		- $
		- $
		- $
		- $
		- $
		- $
		- $
		- $
	Leftover Balance	= $

Weekly Reconciliation	
Flexible Expense Category	**This Week's Spend**
Groceries	$
Household Necessities	$
Self-Care/Wellness	$
Entertainment	$
Outside Food/Drink	$
Other Indulgences	$
Other Transportation	$
Other	$
Total Weekly Spend	$

$ .... + $ .... = $ ....
(Base Daily Budget)   (Yesterday's Leftover Balance)   (Today's Daily Budget)

Day 46		
Flexible Expense Name	**Category**	**Today's Daily Budget:** $ _____
		- $
		- $
		- $
		- $
		- $
		- $
		- $
		- $
	Leftover Balance	**= $**

$ .... + $ .... = $ ....
(Base Daily Budget)   (Yesterday's Leftover Balance)   (Today's Daily Budget)

Day 47		
Flexible Expense Name	**Category**	**Today's Daily Budget:** $ _____
		- $
		- $
		- $
		- $
		- $
		- $
		- $
		- $
	Leftover Balance	**= $**

$ .... + $ .... = $ ....

(Base Daily Budget)   (Yesterday's Leftover Balance)   (Today's Daily Budget)

Day 48		
Flexible Expense Name	**Category**	**Today's Daily Budget:** $ _____
		- $
		- $
		- $
		- $
		- $
		- $
		- $
		- $
	Leftover Balance	= $

$ .... + $ .... = $ ....

(Base Daily Budget)   (Yesterday's Leftover Balance)   (Today's Daily Budget)

Day 49		
Flexible Expense Name	**Category**	**Today's Daily Budget:** $ _____
		- $
		- $
		- $
		- $
		- $
		- $
		- $
		- $
	Leftover Balance	= $

$ .... + $ .... = $ ....
(Base Daily Budget)   (Yesterday's Leftover Balance)   (Today's Daily Budget)

Day 50		
Flexible Expense Name	**Category**	**Today's Daily Budget:** $ _____
		- $
		- $
		- $
		- $
		- $
		- $
		- $
		- $
	Leftover Balance	= $

$ .... + $ .... = $ ....
(Base Daily Budget)   (Yesterday's Leftover Balance)   (Today's Daily Budget)

Day 51		
Flexible Expense Name	**Category**	**Today's Daily Budget:** $ _____
		- $
		- $
		- $
		- $
		- $
		- $
		- $
		- $
	Leftover Balance	= $

$ ....   + $ ....   = $ ....

   (Base Daily Budget)   (Yesterday's Leftover Balance)   (Today's Daily Budget)

Day 52		
Flexible Expense Name	**Category**	**Today's Daily Budget:** $ _____
		- $
		- $
		- $
		- $
		- $
		- $
		- $
		- $
	Leftover Balance	**= $**

Weekly Reconciliation	
Flexible Expense Category	**This Week's Spend**
Groceries	$
Household Necessities	$
Self-Care/Wellness	$
Entertainment	$
Outside Food/Drink	$
Other Indulgences	$
Other Transportation	$
Other	$
Total Weekly Spend	$

$ .... + $ .... = $ ....

Day 53		
Flexible Expense Name	**Category**	**Today's Daily Budget:** $ _____
		- $
		- $
		- $
		- $
		- $
		- $
		- $
		- $
	Leftover Balance	**= $**

$ .... + $ .... = $ ....

Day 54		
Flexible Expense Name	**Category**	**Today's Daily Budget:** $ _____
		- $
		- $
		- $
		- $
		- $
		- $
		- $
		- $
	Leftover Balance	**= $**

$ _____ (Base Daily Budget)   + $ _____ (Yesterday's Leftover Balance)   = $ _____ (Today's Daily Budget)

Day 55		
Flexible Expense Name	**Category**	**Today's Daily Budget:** $ _____
		- $
		- $
		- $
		- $
		- $
		- $
		- $
		- $
	Leftover Balance	**= $**

$ _____ (Base Daily Budget)   + $ _____ (Yesterday's Leftover Balance)   = $ _____ (Today's Daily Budget)

Day 56		
Flexible Expense Name	**Category**	**Today's Daily Budget:** $ _____
		- $
		- $
		- $
		- $
		- $
		- $
		- $
		- $
	Leftover Balance	**= $**

$ .... + $ .... = $ ....

(Base Daily Budget)   (Yesterday's Leftover Balance)   (Today's Daily Budget)

Day 57		
Flexible Expense Name	**Category**	**Today's Daily Budget:** $ _____
		- $
		- $
		- $
		- $
		- $
		- $
		- $
		- $
	Leftover Balance	**= $**

$ .... + $ .... = $ ....

(Base Daily Budget)   (Yesterday's Leftover Balance)   (Today's Daily Budget)

Day 58		
Flexible Expense Name	**Category**	**Today's Daily Budget:** $ _____
		- $
		- $
		- $
		- $
		- $
		- $
		- $
		- $
	Leftover Balance	**= $**

$ _____ + $ _____ = $ _____
....
(Base Daily Budget)   (Yesterday's Leftover Balance)   (Today's Daily Budget)

Day 59		
Flexible Expense Name	**Category**	**Today's Daily Budget:** $ _____
		- $
		- $
		- $
		- $
		- $
		- $
		- $
		- $
	Leftover Balance	**= $**

Weekly Reconciliation	
Flexible Expense Category	**This Week's Spend**
Groceries	$
Household Necessities	$
Self-Care/Wellness	$
Entertainment	$
Outside Food/Drink	$
Other Indulgences	$
Other Transportation	$
Other	$
Total Weekly Spend	$

$ .... + $ .... = $ ....
(Base Daily Budget)   (Yesterday's Leftover Balance)   (Today's Daily Budget)

Day 60		
Flexible Expense Name	**Category**	**Today's Daily Budget:** $ _____
		- $
		- $
		- $
		- $
		- $
		- $
		- $
		- $
	Leftover Balance	= $

$ .... + $ .... = $ ....
(Base Daily Budget)   (Yesterday's Leftover Balance)   (Today's Daily Budget)

Day 61		
Flexible Expense Name	**Category**	**Today's Daily Budget:** $ _____
		- $
		- $
		- $
		- $
		- $
		- $
		- $
		- $
	Leftover Balance	= $

$ .... + $ .... = $ ....

Day 62		
Flexible Expense Name	**Category**	**Today's Daily Budget:** $ _____
		- $
		- $
		- $
		- $
		- $
		- $
		- $
		- $
	Leftover Balance	**= $**

Weekly Reconciliation	
Flexible Expense Category	**This Week's Spend**
Groceries	$
Household Necessities	$
Self-Care/Wellness	$
Entertainment	$
Outside Food/Drink	$
Other Indulgences	$
Other Transportation	$
Other	$
Total Weekly Spend	$

Month 2
Done.

Recapping Last Month

Monthly Reconciliation: **Income**		
Income Category	**Last Month's Forecasted Income**	**Last Month's Actual Income**
Total Active Income	$	$
Total Passive Income	$	$
Any Other Income	$	$
Total Monthly Income	$	$

(You can easily get your "Actual Amount Spent Last Month" values by summing up the "Total Weekly Spend" values in your weekly reconciliations)

Monthly Reconciliation: **Flexible Expenses**		
Flexible Expense Category	**Last Month's Budget**	**Actual Amount Spent Last Month**
Groceries	$	$
Household Necessities	$	$
Self-Care/Wellness	$	$
Entertainment	$	$
Outside Food/Drink	$	$
Other Indulgences	$	$
Other Transportation	$	$
Other	$	$
Total Monthly Flexible Expenses	$	$

Monthly Reconciliation: __Fixed Expenses__

Fixed Expense Category	Last Month's Budget	Actual Amount Spent Last Month
Rent/Mortgage	$	$
Bills	$	$
Car Payments	$	$
Insurance	$	$
Subscriptions	$	$
Other	$	$
Total Monthly Fixed Expenses	$	$

Monthly Reconciliation: __Debt Balance__

Debt Name	Beginning of Last Month Balance	Amount Budgeted For Last Month	Actual Amount Paid Last Month	Remaining Debt Balance
	$	$	$	$
	$	$	$	$
	$	$	$	$
	$	$	$	$
	$	$	$	$
	$	$	$	$
	$	$	$	$
	$	$	$	$
	$	$	$	$
	$	$	$	$
Debt Totals	$	$	$	$

Recap Questions

1. What did I overspend on unnecessarily this month?
   Why do I think that happened?

....

....

....

2. What adjustments do I need to make to my spending
   to set my future self up in a much better position?

....

....

....

3. What emotional impulses am I letting lead my spending habits?
   If I had ultimate willpower, what would I change in regards
   to my spending?

....

....

....

4. What have I learned about myself in relation to money? What
   specific actions can I take to improve based on what I've learned?

....

....

....

Month 3

Days
63 - 93

Monthly Budget Preparation

My main financial goal for the month:

This Month's Forecast: <u>Income</u>

Income Category	Forecasted Amount
Total Active Income	$
Total Passive Income	$
Any Other Income	$
This Month's Forecasted Income	$

This Month's Budget: <u>Fixed Expenses</u>

Fixed Expense Category	Budget
Rent/Mortgage	$
Bills	$
Car Payments	$
Insurance	$
Subscriptions	$
Other	$
This Month's Fixed Expense Budget	$

<u>Debt Clearing Planner</u>

Debt Name	Total Balance Remaining	Budget	Total Month's Remaining to Complete
	$	$	
	$	$	
	$	$	
	$	$	
	$	$	
	$	$	
	$	$	
	$	$	
	$	$	
	$	$	
This Month's Debt Budget			

$ _____   − $ _____   − $ _____

(This Month's   (This Month's   (This Month's
Forecasted Income)   Fixed Expense Budget)   Debt Budget)

= $ _____

(This Month's
Remaining Balance)

1. Now, choose how to allocate this remaining balance based on your personalized goals.

Note: These two fields' totals should add up to "This Month's Remaining Balance."

$ _____ $ _____

(This Month's   (This Month's Flexible
Savings Goal)   Expense Budget)

2. Next, take "This Month's Flexible Expense Budget" and break it down based on the following categories:

This Month's Budget: **Flexible Expenses**	
Flexible Expense Category	**This Month's Budget**
Groceries	$
Household Necessities	$
Self-Care/Wellness	$
Entertainment	$
Outside Food/Drink	$
Other Indulgences	$
Other Transportation	$
Other	$
This Month's Flexible Expense Budget	$

3. Lastly, we'll calculate the daily budget you need to adhere to in order to achieve your monthly budgeting goal:

$ _____   ÷   _____   = $ _____

(This Month's Flexible   (Total Days In   (Base Daily Budget)
Expense Budget)   Upcoming Month)

_____ , 20 ___

(This is an optional tool you can use to help get a visual overview of your entire month)

Mon	Tue	Wed	Thu	Fri	Sat	Sun

$ .... + $ .... = $ ....
(Base Daily Budget)   (Yesterday's Leftover Balance)   (Today's Daily Budget)

Day 63		
Flexible Expense Name	**Category**	**Today's Daily Budget:** $ _____
		- $
		- $
		- $
		- $
		- $
		- $
		- $
		- $
	Leftover Balance	**= $**

$ .... + $ .... = $ ....
(Base Daily Budget)   (Yesterday's Leftover Balance)   (Today's Daily Budget)

Day 64		
Flexible Expense Name	**Category**	**Today's Daily Budget:** $ _____
		- $
		- $
		- $
		- $
		- $
		- $
		- $
		- $
	Leftover Balance	**= $**

$ .... + $ .... = $ ....
(Base Daily Budget) *(Yesterday's Leftover Balance)* *(Today's Daily Budget)*

Day 65		
Flexible Expense Name	**Category**	**Today's Daily Budget:** $ _____
		- $
		- $
		- $
		- $
		- $
		- $
		- $
		- $
	Leftover Balance	= $

$ .... + $ .... = $ ....
(Base Daily Budget) *(Yesterday's Leftover Balance)* *(Today's Daily Budget)*

Day 66		
Flexible Expense Name	**Category**	**Today's Daily Budget:** $ _____
		- $
		- $
		- $
		- $
		- $
		- $
		- $
		- $
	Leftover Balance	= $

$ ....   + $ ....   = $ ....

(Base Daily Budget)   (Yesterday's Leftover Balance)   (Today's Daily Budget)

Day 67		
Flexible Expense Name	**Category**	**Today's Daily Budget:** $ _____
		- $
		- $
		- $
		- $
		- $
		- $
		- $
		- $
	Leftover Balance	**= $**

$ ....   + $ ....   = $ ....

(Base Daily Budget)   (Yesterday's Leftover Balance)   (Today's Daily Budget)

Day 68		
Flexible Expense Name	**Category**	**Today's Daily Budget:** $ _____
		- $
		- $
		- $
		- $
		- $
		- $
		- $
		- $
	Leftover Balance	**= $**

$ .... + $ .... = $ ....

(Base Daily Budget)   (Yesterday's Leftover Balance)   (Today's Daily Budget)

Day 69		
Flexible Expense Name	**Category**	**Today's Daily Budget:** $ _____
		- $
		- $
		- $
		- $
		- $
		- $
		- $
		- $
	Leftover Balance	**= $**

Weekly Reconciliation	
Flexible Expense Category	**This Week's Spend**
Groceries	$
Household Necessities	$
Self-Care/Wellness	$
Entertainment	$
Outside Food/Drink	$
Other Indulgences	$
Other Transportation	$
Other	$
Total Weekly Spend	$

$ .... + $ .... = $ ....
(Base Daily Budget)   (Yesterday's Leftover Balance)   (Today's Daily Budget)

Day 70		
Flexible Expense Name	**Category**	**Today's Daily Budget:** $ _____
		- $
		- $
		- $
		- $
		- $
		- $
		- $
		- $
	Leftover Balance	**= $**

$ .... + $ .... = $ ....
(Base Daily Budget)   (Yesterday's Leftover Balance)   (Today's Daily Budget)

Day 71		
Flexible Expense Name	**Category**	**Today's Daily Budget:** $ _____
		- $
		- $
		- $
		- $
		- $
		- $
		- $
		- $
	Leftover Balance	**= $**

$ .... + $ .... = $ ....
(Base Daily Budget)   (Yesterday's Leftover Balance)   (Today's Daily Budget)

Day 72		
Flexible Expense Name	**Category**	**Today's Daily Budget:** $ _____
		- $
		- $
		- $
		- $
		- $
		- $
		- $
		- $
	Leftover Balance	= $

$ .... + $ .... = $ ....
(Base Daily Budget)   (Yesterday's Leftover Balance)   (Today's Daily Budget)

Day 73		
Flexible Expense Name	**Category**	**Today's Daily Budget:** $ _____
		- $
		- $
		- $
		- $
		- $
		- $
		- $
		- $
	Leftover Balance	= $

$ .... + $ .... = $ ....
(Base Daily Budget)   (Yesterday's Leftover Balance)   (Today's Daily Budget)

Day 74		
Flexible Expense Name	**Category**	**Today's Daily Budget:** $ _____
		- $
		- $
		- $
		- $
		- $
		- $
		- $
		- $
	Leftover Balance	= $

$ .... + $ .... = $ ....
(Base Daily Budget)   (Yesterday's Leftover Balance)   (Today's Daily Budget)

Day 75		
Flexible Expense Name	**Category**	**Today's Daily Budget:** $ _____
		- $
		- $
		- $
		- $
		- $
		- $
		- $
		- $
	Leftover Balance	= $

$ .... + $ .... = $ ....
(Base Daily Budget)   (Yesterday's Leftover Balance)   (Today's Daily Budget)

Day 76		
Flexible Expense Name	**Category**	**Today's Daily Budget:** $ _____
		- $
		- $
		- $
		- $
		- $
		- $
		- $
		- $
	Leftover Balance	**= $**

Weekly Reconciliation	
Flexible Expense Category	**This Week's Spend**
Groceries	$
Household Necessities	$
Self-Care/Wellness	$
Entertainment	$
Outside Food/Drink	$
Other Indulgences	$
Other Transportation	$
Other	$
Total Weekly Spend	$

$ .... + $ .... = $ ....
(Base Daily Budget)   (Yesterday's Leftover Balance)   (Today's Daily Budget)

Day 77		
Flexible Expense Name	**Category**	**Today's Daily Budget:** $ _____
		- $
		- $
		- $
		- $
		- $
		- $
		- $
		- $
	Leftover Balance	= $

$ .... + $ .... = $ ....
(Base Daily Budget)   (Yesterday's Leftover Balance)   (Today's Daily Budget)

Day 78		
Flexible Expense Name	**Category**	**Today's Daily Budget:** $ _____
		- $
		- $
		- $
		- $
		- $
		- $
		- $
		- $
	Leftover Balance	= $

$ .... + $ .... = $ ....
(Base Daily Budget)   (Yesterday's Leftover Balance)   (Today's Daily Budget)

Day 79		
Flexible Expense Name	**Category**	**Today's Daily Budget:** $ _____
		- $
		- $
		- $
		- $
		- $
		- $
		- $
		- $
	Leftover Balance	= $

$ .... + $ .... = $ ....
(Base Daily Budget)   (Yesterday's Leftover Balance)   (Today's Daily Budget)

Day 80		
Flexible Expense Name	**Category**	**Today's Daily Budget:** $ _____
		- $
		- $
		- $
		- $
		- $
		- $
		- $
		- $
	Leftover Balance	= $

$ .... + $ .... = $ ....
(Base Daily Budget)   (Yesterday's Leftover Balance)   (Today's Daily Budget)

Day 81		
Flexible Expense Name	**Category**	**Today's Daily Budget:** $ _____
		- $
		- $
		- $
		- $
		- $
		- $
		- $
		- $
	Leftover Balance	= $

$ .... + $ .... = $ ....
(Base Daily Budget)   (Yesterday's Leftover Balance)   (Today's Daily Budget)

Day 82		
Flexible Expense Name	**Category**	**Today's Daily Budget:** $ _____
		- $
		- $
		- $
		- $
		- $
		- $
		- $
		- $
	Leftover Balance	= $

$ _____ + $ _____ = $ _____

(Base Daily Budget)   (Yesterday's Leftover Balance)   (Today's Daily Budget)

Day 83		
Flexible Expense Name	**Category**	**Today's Daily Budget:** $ _____
		– $
		– $
		– $
		– $
		– $
		– $
		– $
		– $
	Leftover Balance	**= $**

Weekly Reconciliation	
Flexible Expense Category	**This Week's Spend**
Groceries	$
Household Necessities	$
Self-Care/Wellness	$
Entertainment	$
Outside Food/Drink	$
Other Indulgences	$
Other Transportation	$
Other	$
Total Weekly Spend	$

$ .... + $ .... = $ ....
(Base Daily Budget)   (Yesterday's Leftover Balance)   (Today's Daily Budget)

Day 84		
Flexible Expense Name	**Category**	**Today's Daily Budget:** $ _____
		- $
		- $
		- $
		- $
		- $
		- $
		- $
		- $
	Leftover Balance	= $

$ .... + $ .... = $ ....
(Base Daily Budget)   (Yesterday's Leftover Balance)   (Today's Daily Budget)

Day 85		
Flexible Expense Name	**Category**	**Today's Daily Budget:** $ _____
		- $
		- $
		- $
		- $
		- $
		- $
		- $
		- $
	Leftover Balance	= $

$ .... + $ .... = $ ....
(Base Daily Budget)   (Yesterday's Leftover Balance)   (Today's Daily Budget)

Day 86		
Flexible Expense Name	**Category**	**Today's Daily Budget:** $ _____
		- $
		- $
		- $
		- $
		- $
		- $
		- $
		- $
	Leftover Balance	**= $**

$ .... + $ .... = $ ....
(Base Daily Budget)   (Yesterday's Leftover Balance)   (Today's Daily Budget)

Day 87		
Flexible Expense Name	**Category**	**Today's Daily Budget:** $ _____
		- $
		- $
		- $
		- $
		- $
		- $
		- $
		- $
	Leftover Balance	**= $**

$ .... + $ .... = $ ....
(Base Daily Budget)   (Yesterday's Leftover Balance)   (Today's Daily Budget)

Day 88		
Flexible Expense Name	**Category**	**Today's Daily Budget:** $ _____
		- $
		- $
		- $
		- $
		- $
		- $
		- $
		- $
	Leftover Balance	**= $**

$ .... + $ .... = $ ....
(Base Daily Budget)   (Yesterday's Leftover Balance)   (Today's Daily Budget)

Day 89		
Flexible Expense Name	**Category**	**Today's Daily Budget:** $ _____
		- $
		- $
		- $
		- $
		- $
		- $
		- $
		- $
	Leftover Balance	**= $**

$ .... + $ .... = $ ....

(Base Daily Budget)   (Yesterday's Leftover Balance)   (Today's Daily Budget)

Day 90		
Flexible Expense Name	**Category**	**Today's Daily Budget:** $ _____
		- $
		- $
		- $
		- $
		- $
		- $
		- $
		- $
	Leftover Balance	**= $**

Weekly Reconciliation	
Flexible Expense Category	**This Week's Spend**
Groceries	$
Household Necessities	$
Self-Care/Wellness	$
Entertainment	$
Outside Food/Drink	$
Other Indulgences	$
Other Transportation	$
Other	$
Total Weekly Spend	$

$ .... + $ .... = $ ....
(Base Daily Budget)   (Yesterday's Leftover Balance)   (Today's Daily Budget)

Day 91		
Flexible Expense Name	**Category**	**Today's Daily Budget:** $ _____
		- $
		- $
		- $
		- $
		- $
		- $
		- $
		- $
	Leftover Balance	= $

$ .... + $ .... = $ ....
(Base Daily Budget)   (Yesterday's Leftover Balance)   (Today's Daily Budget)

Day 92		
Flexible Expense Name	**Category**	**Today's Daily Budget:** $ _____
		- $
		- $
		- $
		- $
		- $
		- $
		- $
		- $
	Leftover Balance	= $

$ .... + $ .... = $ ....

(Base Daily Budget)   (Yesterday's Leftover Balance)   (Today's Daily Budget)

Day 93		
Flexible Expense Name	**Category**	**Today's Daily Budget:** $ _____
		- $
		- $
		- $
		- $
		- $
		- $
		- $
		- $
	Leftover Balance	**= $**

Weekly Reconciliation	
Flexible Expense Category	**This Week's Spend**
Groceries	$
Household Necessities	$
Self-Care/Wellness	$
Entertainment	$
Outside Food/Drink	$
Other Indulgences	$
Other Transportation	$
Other	$
Total Weekly Spend	$

Month 3

Done.

Recapping Last Month

Monthly Reconciliation: <u>Income</u>		
Income Category	**Last Month's Forecasted Income**	**Last Month's Actual Income**
Total Active Income	$	$
Total Passive Income	$	$
Any Other Income	$	$
Total Monthly Income	$	$

(You can easily get your "Actual Amount Spent Last Month" values by summing up the "Total Weekly Spend" values in your weekly reconciliations)

Monthly Reconciliation: <u>Flexible Expenses</u>		
Flexible Expense Category	**Last Month's Budget**	**Actual Amount Spent Last Month**
Groceries	$	$
Household Necessities	$	$
Self-Care/Wellness	$	$
Entertainment	$	$
Outside Food/Drink	$	$
Other Indulgences	$	$
Other Transportation	$	$
Other	$	$
Total Monthly Flexible Expenses	$	$

Monthly Reconciliation: **Fixed Expenses**

Fixed Expense Category	Last Month's Budget	Actual Amount Spent Last Month
Rent/Mortgage	$	$
Bills	$	$
Car Payments	$	$
Insurance	$	$
Subscriptions	$	$
Other	$	$
Total Monthly Fixed Expenses	$	$

Monthly Reconciliation: **Debt Balance**

Debt Name	Beginning of Last Month Balance	Amount Budgeted For Last Month	Actual Amount Paid Last Month	Remaining Debt Balance
	$	$	$	$
	$	$	$	$
	$	$	$	$
	$	$	$	$
	$	$	$	$
	$	$	$	$
	$	$	$	$
	$	$	$	$
	$	$	$	$
	$	$	$	$
Debt Totals	$	$	$	$

Recap Questions

1. What did I overspend on unnecessarily this month?
   Why do I think that happened?

....

....

....

2. What adjustments do I need to make to my spending
   to set my future self up in a much better position?

....

....

....

3. Look at the amount you saved (or didn't save)
   this month— how do you feel about where you ended up?

....

....

....

4. If I continue along this journey, what future opportunities
   open up for me based on my savings goals?

....

....

....

Month 4
Days
94 - 124

Monthly Budget Preparation

My main financial goal for the month:

This Month's Forecast: **Income**

Income Category	Forecasted Amount
Total Active Income	$
Total Passive Income	$
Any Other Income	$
This Month's Forecasted Income	$

This Month's Budget: **Fixed Expenses**

Fixed Expense Category	Budget
Rent/Mortgage	$
Bills	$
Car Payments	$
Insurance	$
Subscriptions	$
Other	$
This Month's Fixed Expense Budget	$

Debt Clearing Planner

Debt Name	Total Balance Remaining	Budget	Total Month's Remaining to Complete
	$	$	
	$	$	
	$	$	
	$	$	
	$	$	
	$	$	
	$	$	
	$	$	
	$	$	
	$	$	
This Month's Debt Budget			

$ _____   − $ _____   − $ _____

(This Month's
Forecasted Income)

(This Month's
Fixed Expense Budget)

(This Month's
Debt Budget)

= $ _____

(This Month's
Remaining Balance)

1. Now, choose how to allocate this remaining balance based on your personalized goals.

Note: These two fields' totals should add up to "This Month's Remaining Balance."

$ _____ $ _____

(This Month's
Savings Goal)

(This Month's Flexible
Expense Budget)

2. Next, take "This Month's Flexible Expense Budget" and break it down based on the following categories:

This Month's Budget: **Flexible Expenses**	
Flexible Expense Category	**This Month's Budget**
Groceries	$
Household Necessities	$
Self-Care/Wellness	$
Entertainment	$
Outside Food/Drink	$
Other Indulgences	$
Other Transportation	$
Other	$
This Month's Flexible Expense Budget	$

3. Lastly, we'll calculate the daily budget you need to adhere to in order to achieve your monthly budgeting goal:

$ _____   ÷   _____   = $ _____

(This Month's Flexible
Expense Budget)

(Total Days In
Upcoming Month)

(Base Daily Budget)

_____ , 20 ___

(This is an optional tool you can use to help get a visual overview of your entire month)

Mon	Tue	Wed	Thu	Fri	Sat	Sun

$ .... + $ .... = $ ....

(Base Daily Budget)   (Yesterday's Leftover Balance)   (Today's Daily Budget)

Day 94		
Flexible Expense Name	**Category**	**Today's Daily Budget:** $ _____
		- $
		- $
		- $
		- $
		- $
		- $
		- $
		- $
	Leftover Balance	= $

$ .... + $ .... = $ ....

(Base Daily Budget)   (Yesterday's Leftover Balance)   (Today's Daily Budget)

Day 95		
Flexible Expense Name	**Category**	**Today's Daily Budget:** $ _____
		- $
		- $
		- $
		- $
		- $
		- $
		- $
		- $
	Leftover Balance	= $

$ .... + $ .... = $ ....
(Base Daily Budget)   (Yesterday's Leftover Balance)   (Today's Daily Budget)

Day 96		
Flexible Expense Name	**Category**	**Today's Daily Budget:** $ _____
		- $
		- $
		- $
		- $
		- $
		- $
		- $
		- $
	Leftover Balance	**= $**

$ .... + $ .... = $ ....
(Base Daily Budget)   (Yesterday's Leftover Balance)   (Today's Daily Budget)

Day 97		
Flexible Expense Name	**Category**	**Today's Daily Budget:** $ _____
		- $
		- $
		- $
		- $
		- $
		- $
		- $
		- $
	Leftover Balance	**= $**

$ .... + $ .... = $ ....
(Base Daily Budget)   (Yesterday's Leftover Balance)   (Today's Daily Budget)

Day 98		
Flexible Expense Name	**Category**	**Today's Daily Budget:** $ _____
		– $
		– $
		– $
		– $
		– $
		– $
		– $
		– $
	Leftover Balance	**= $**

$ .... + $ .... = $ ....
(Base Daily Budget)   (Yesterday's Leftover Balance)   (Today's Daily Budget)

Day 99		
Flexible Expense Name	**Category**	**Today's Daily Budget:** $ _____
		– $
		– $
		– $
		– $
		– $
		– $
		– $
		– $
	Leftover Balance	**= $**

$ _____ + $ _____ = $ _____
(Base Daily Budget)   (Yesterday's Leftover Balance)   (Today's Daily Budget)

Day 100		
Flexible Expense Name	**Category**	**Today's Daily Budget:** $ _____
		- $
		- $
		- $
		- $
		- $
		- $
		- $
		- $
	Leftover Balance	= $

Weekly Reconciliation	
Flexible Expense Category	**This Week's Spend**
Groceries	$
Household Necessities	$
Self-Care/Wellness	$
Entertainment	$
Outside Food/Drink	$
Other Indulgences	$
Other Transportation	$
Other	$
Total Weekly Spend	$

$ .... + $ .... = $ ....
(Base Daily Budget)   (Yesterday's Leftover Balance)   (Today's Daily Budget)

Day 101		
Flexible Expense Name	**Category**	**Today's Daily Budget:** $ _____
		- $
		- $
		- $
		- $
		- $
		- $
		- $
		- $
	Leftover Balance	= $

$ .... + $ .... = $ ....
(Base Daily Budget)   (Yesterday's Leftover Balance)   (Today's Daily Budget)

Day 102		
Flexible Expense Name	**Category**	**Today's Daily Budget:** $ _____
		- $
		- $
		- $
		- $
		- $
		- $
		- $
		- $
	Leftover Balance	= $

$ .... + $ .... = $ ....

Day 103		
Flexible Expense Name	**Category**	**Today's Daily Budget:** $ _____
		– $
		– $
		– $
		– $
		– $
		– $
		– $
		– $
	Leftover Balance	**= $**

$ .... + $ .... = $ ....

Day 104		
Flexible Expense Name	**Category**	**Today's Daily Budget:** $ _____
		– $
		– $
		– $
		– $
		– $
		– $
		– $
		– $
	Leftover Balance	**= $**

$ .... + $ .... = $ ....
(Base Daily Budget)   (Yesterday's Leftover Balance)   (Today's Daily Budget)

Day 105		
Flexible Expense Name	**Category**	**Today's Daily Budget:** $ _____
		- $
		- $
		- $
		- $
		- $
		- $
		- $
		- $
	Leftover Balance	**= $**

$ .... + $ .... = $ ....
(Base Daily Budget)   (Yesterday's Leftover Balance)   (Today's Daily Budget)

Day 106		
Flexible Expense Name	**Category**	**Today's Daily Budget:** $ _____
		- $
		- $
		- $
		- $
		- $
		- $
		- $
		- $
	Leftover Balance	**= $**

$ _____ + $ _____ = $ _____
(Base Daily Budget)   (Yesterday's Leftover Balance)   (Today's Daily Budget)

Day 107		
Flexible Expense Name	**Category**	**Today's Daily Budget:** $ _____
		- $
		- $
		- $
		- $
		- $
		- $
		- $
		- $
	Leftover Balance	= $

Weekly Reconciliation	
Flexible Expense Category	**This Week's Spend**
Groceries	$
Household Necessities	$
Self-Care/Wellness	$
Entertainment	$
Outside Food/Drink	$
Other Indulgences	$
Other Transportation	$
Other	$
Total Weekly Spend	$

$ .... + $ .... = $ ....
(Base Daily Budget)   (Yesterday's Leftover Balance)   (Today's Daily Budget)

Day 108		
Flexible Expense Name	**Category**	**Today's Daily Budget:** $ _____
		- $
		- $
		- $
		- $
		- $
		- $
		- $
		- $
	Leftover Balance	**= $**

$ .... + $ .... = $ ....
(Base Daily Budget)   (Yesterday's Leftover Balance)   (Today's Daily Budget)

Day 109		
Flexible Expense Name	**Category**	**Today's Daily Budget:** $ _____
		- $
		- $
		- $
		- $
		- $
		- $
		- $
		- $
	Leftover Balance	**= $**

$ .... + $ .... = $ ....
 (Base Daily Budget)   (Yesterday's Leftover Balance)   (Today's Daily Budget)

Day 110		
Flexible Expense Name	**Category**	**Today's Daily Budget:** **$** _____
		- $
		- $
		- $
		- $
		- $
		- $
		- $
		- $
	Leftover Balance	**= $**

$ .... + $ .... = $ ....
 (Base Daily Budget)   (Yesterday's Leftover Balance)   (Today's Daily Budget)

Day 111		
Flexible Expense Name	**Category**	**Today's Daily Budget:** **$** _____
		- $
		- $
		- $
		- $
		- $
		- $
		- $
		- $
	Leftover Balance	**= $**

$ .... (Base Daily Budget)   + $ .... (Yesterday's Leftover Balance)   = $ .... (Today's Daily Budget)

Day 112		
Flexible Expense Name	**Category**	**Today's Daily Budget:** $ _____
		- $
		- $
		- $
		- $
		- $
		- $
		- $
		- $
	Leftover Balance	= $

$ .... (Base Daily Budget)   + $ .... (Yesterday's Leftover Balance)   = $ .... (Today's Daily Budget)

Day 113		
Flexible Expense Name	**Category**	**Today's Daily Budget:** $ _____
		- $
		- $
		- $
		- $
		- $
		- $
		- $
		- $
	Leftover Balance	= $

$ .... (Base Daily Budget)   + $ .... (Yesterday's Leftover Balance)   = $ .... (Today's Daily Budget)

Day 114		
Flexible Expense Name	**Category**	**Today's Daily Budget:** $ _____
		- $
		- $
		- $
		- $
		- $
		- $
		- $
		- $
	Leftover Balance	**= $**

Weekly Reconciliation	
Flexible Expense Category	**This Week's Spend**
Groceries	$
Household Necessities	$
Self-Care/Wellness	$
Entertainment	$
Outside Food/Drink	$
Other Indulgences	$
Other Transportation	$
Other	$
Total Weekly Spend	$

$ ....   + $ ....   = $ ....

(Base Daily Budget)   (Yesterday's Leftover Balance)   (Today's Daily Budget)

Day 115		
Flexible Expense Name	**Category**	**Today's Daily Budget:** $ _____
		- $
		- $
		- $
		- $
		- $
		- $
		- $
		- $
	Leftover Balance	**= $**

$ ....   + $ ....   = $ ....

(Base Daily Budget)   (Yesterday's Leftover Balance)   (Today's Daily Budget)

Day 116		
Flexible Expense Name	**Category**	**Today's Daily Budget:** $ _____
		- $
		- $
		- $
		- $
		- $
		- $
		- $
		- $
	Leftover Balance	**= $**

$ .... + $ .... = $ ....
(Base Daily Budget)   *(Yesterday's Leftover Balance)*   *(Today's Daily Budget)*

Day 117		
Flexible Expense Name	**Category**	**Today's Daily Budget:** $ _____
		- $
		- $
		- $
		- $
		- $
		- $
		- $
		- $
	Leftover Balance	**= $**

$ .... + $ .... = $ ....
(Base Daily Budget)   *(Yesterday's Leftover Balance)*   *(Today's Daily Budget)*

Day 118		
Flexible Expense Name	**Category**	**Today's Daily Budget:** $ _____
		- $
		- $
		- $
		- $
		- $
		- $
		- $
		- $
	Leftover Balance	**= $**

$ .... + $ .... = $ ....
(Base Daily Budget)   (Yesterday's Leftover Balance)   (Today's Daily Budget)

Day 119		
Flexible Expense Name	**Category**	**Today's Daily Budget:** $ _____
		- $
		- $
		- $
		- $
		- $
		- $
		- $
		- $
	Leftover Balance	**= $**

$ .... + $ .... = $ ....
(Base Daily Budget)   (Yesterday's Leftover Balance)   (Today's Daily Budget)

Day 120		
Flexible Expense Name	**Category**	**Today's Daily Budget:** $ _____
		- $
		- $
		- $
		- $
		- $
		- $
		- $
		- $
	Leftover Balance	**= $**

$ .... + $ .... = $ ....

(Base Daily Budget)   (Yesterday's Leftover Balance)   (Today's Daily Budget)

Day 121		
Flexible Expense Name	**Category**	**Today's Daily Budget:** $ _____
		- $
		- $
		- $
		- $
		- $
		- $
		- $
		- $
	Leftover Balance	**= $**

Weekly Reconciliation	
Flexible Expense Category	**This Week's Spend**
Groceries	$
Household Necessities	$
Self-Care/Wellness	$
Entertainment	$
Outside Food/Drink	$
Other Indulgences	$
Other Transportation	$
Other	$
Total Weekly Spend	$

$ .... + $ .... = $ ....
(Base Daily Budget)   (Yesterday's Leftover Balance)   (Today's Daily Budget)

Day 122		
Flexible Expense Name	**Category**	**Today's Daily Budget:** $ _____
		- $
		- $
		- $
		- $
		- $
		- $
		- $
		- $
	Leftover Balance	**= $**

$ .... + $ .... = $ ....
(Base Daily Budget)   (Yesterday's Leftover Balance)   (Today's Daily Budget)

Day 123		
Flexible Expense Name	**Category**	**Today's Daily Budget:** $ _____
		- $
		- $
		- $
		- $
		- $
		- $
		- $
		- $
	Leftover Balance	**= $**

$ _____ + $ _____ = $ _____
(Base Daily Budget)   (Yesterday's Leftover Balance)   (Today's Daily Budget)

Day 124		
Flexible Expense Name	**Category**	**Today's Daily Budget:** $ _____
		– $
		– $
		– $
		– $
		– $
		– $
		– $
		– $
	Leftover Balance	**= $**

Weekly Reconciliation	
Flexible Expense Category	**This Week's Spend**
Groceries	$
Household Necessities	$
Self-Care/Wellness	$
Entertainment	$
Outside Food/Drink	$
Other Indulgences	$
Other Transportation	$
Other	$
Total Weekly Spend	$

Month 4
Done.

Recapping Last Month

Income Category	Last Month's Forecasted Income	Last Month's Actual Income
Total Active Income	$	$
Total Passive Income	$	$
Any Other Income	$	$
Total Monthly Income	$	$

(You can easily get your "Actual Amount Spent Last Month" values by summing up the "Total Weekly Spend" values in your weekly reconciliations)

Monthly Reconciliation: **Flexible Expenses**

Flexible Expense Category	Last Month's Budget	Actual Amount Spent Last Month
Groceries	$	$
Household Necessities	$	$
Self-Care/Wellness	$	$
Entertainment	$	$
Outside Food/Drink	$	$
Other Indulgences	$	$
Other Transportation	$	$
Other	$	$
Total Monthly Flexible Expenses	$	$

Monthly Reconciliation: **Fixed Expenses**

Fixed Expense Category	Last Month's Budget	Actual Amount Spent Last Month
Rent/Mortgage	$	$
Bills	$	$
Car Payments	$	$
Insurance	$	$
Subscriptions	$	$
Other	$	$
Total Monthly Fixed Expenses	$	$

Monthly Reconciliation: **Debt Balance**

Debt Name	Beginning of Last Month Balance	Amount Budgeted For Last Month	Actual Amount Paid Last Month	Remaining Debt Balance
	$	$	$	$
	$	$	$	$
	$	$	$	$
	$	$	$	$
	$	$	$	$
	$	$	$	$
	$	$	$	$
	$	$	$	$
	$	$	$	$
	$	$	$	$
Debt Totals	$	$	$	$

Recap Questions

1. What did I overspend on unnecessarily this month?
   Why do I think that happened?

....

....

....

2. What adjustments do I need to make to my spending
   to set my future self up in a much better position?

....

....

....

3. What will I tell myself if I spend over my daily budget one day?
   What actions will I take the following day(s) to get back on track?

....

....

....

4. In what ways can I be more supportive and forgiving of
   myself on this journey? How am I being too hard on myself?

....

....

....

Month 5
Days
125 - 155

Monthly Budget Preparation

My main financial goal for the month:

This Month's Forecast: **Income**

Income Category	Forecasted Amount
Total Active Income	$
Total Passive Income	$
Any Other Income	$
This Month's Forecasted Income	$

This Month's Budget: **Fixed Expenses**

Fixed Expense Category	Budget
Rent/Mortgage	$
Bills	$
Car Payments	$
Insurance	$
Subscriptions	$
Other	$
This Month's Fixed Expense Budget	$

Debt Clearing Planner

Debt Name	Total Balance Remaining	Budget	Total Month's Remaining to Complete
	$	$	
	$	$	
	$	$	
	$	$	
	$	$	
	$	$	
	$	$	
	$	$	
	$	$	
	$	$	
This Month's Debt Budget			

$ _____   − $ _____   − $ _____

(This Month's
Forecasted Income)
        (This Month's
Fixed Expense Budget)
        (This Month's
Debt Budget)

= $ _____

(This Month's
Remaining Balance)

1. Now, choose how to allocate this remaining balance based on your personalized goals.

Note: These two fields' totals should add up to "This Month's Remaining Balance."

$ _____ $ _____

(This Month's
Savings Goal)
        (This Month's Flexible
Expense Budget)

2. Next, take "This Month's Flexible Expense Budget" and break it down based on the following categories:

This Month's Budget: **Flexible Expenses**	
Flexible Expense Category	**This Month's Budget**
Groceries	$
Household Necessities	$
Self-Care/Wellness	$
Entertainment	$
Outside Food/Drink	$
Other Indulgences	$
Other Transportation	$
Other	$
This Month's Flexible Expense Budget	$

3. Lastly, we'll calculate the daily budget you need to adhere to in order to achieve your monthly budgeting goal:

$ _____   ÷ $ _____   = $ _____

(This Month's Flexible
Expense Budget)
        (Total Days In
Upcoming Month)
        (Base Daily Budget)

_____ , 20 ___

(Month)　　　　　　　(Year)

(This is an optional tool you can use to help
get a visual overview of your entire month)

Mon	Tue	Wed	Thu	Fri	Sat	Sun

$ .... + $ .... = $ ....
(Base Daily Budget)   (Yesterday's Leftover Balance)   (Today's Daily Budget)

Day 125		
Flexible Expense Name	**Category**	**Today's Daily Budget:** $ _____
		- $
		- $
		- $
		- $
		- $
		- $
		- $
		- $
	Leftover Balance	= $

$ .... + $ .... = $ ....
(Base Daily Budget)   (Yesterday's Leftover Balance)   (Today's Daily Budget)

Day 126		
Flexible Expense Name	**Category**	**Today's Daily Budget:** $ _____
		- $
		- $
		- $
		- $
		- $
		- $
		- $
		- $
	Leftover Balance	= $

$ _____   + $ _____   = $ _____

(Base Daily Budget)   (Yesterday's Leftover Balance)   (Today's Daily Budget)

Day 127		
Flexible Expense Name	**Category**	**Today's Daily Budget:** $ _____
		- $
		- $
		- $
		- $
		- $
		- $
		- $
		- $
	Leftover Balance	**= $**

$ _____   + $ _____   = $ _____

(Base Daily Budget)   (Yesterday's Leftover Balance)   (Today's Daily Budget)

Day 128		
Flexible Expense Name	**Category**	**Today's Daily Budget:** $ _____
		- $
		- $
		- $
		- $
		- $
		- $
		- $
		- $
	Leftover Balance	**= $**

$ .... + $ .... = $ ....
(Base Daily Budget)　　　(Yesterday's Leftover Balance)　　　(Today's Daily Budget)

Day 129		
Flexible Expense Name	**Category**	**Today's Daily Budget:** $ _____
		- $
		- $
		- $
		- $
		- $
		- $
		- $
		- $
	Leftover Balance	= $

$ .... + $ .... = $ ....
(Base Daily Budget)　　　(Yesterday's Leftover Balance)　　　(Today's Daily Budget)

Day 130		
Flexible Expense Name	**Category**	**Today's Daily Budget:** $ _____
		- $
		- $
		- $
		- $
		- $
		- $
		- $
		- $
	Leftover Balance	= $

$ .... + $ .... = $ ....
(Base Daily Budget)   (Yesterday's Leftover Balance)   (Today's Daily Budget)

Day 131		
Flexible Expense Name	**Category**	**Today's Daily Budget:** $ _____
		- $
		- $
		- $
		- $
		- $
		- $
		- $
		- $
	Leftover Balance	**= $**

Weekly Reconciliation	
Flexible Expense Category	**This Week's Spend**
Groceries	$
Household Necessities	$
Self-Care/Wellness	$
Entertainment	$
Outside Food/Drink	$
Other Indulgences	$
Other Transportation	$
Other	$
Total Weekly Spend	$

$ .... + $ .... = $ ....
(Base Daily Budget)   (Yesterday's Leftover Balance)   (Today's Daily Budget)

Day 132		
Flexible Expense Name	**Category**	**Today's Daily Budget:** $ _____
		- $
		- $
		- $
		- $
		- $
		- $
		- $
		- $
	Leftover Balance	= $

$ .... + $ .... = $ ....
(Base Daily Budget)   (Yesterday's Leftover Balance)   (Today's Daily Budget)

Day 133		
Flexible Expense Name	**Category**	**Today's Daily Budget:** $ _____
		- $
		- $
		- $
		- $
		- $
		- $
		- $
		- $
	Leftover Balance	= $

$ ....   + $ ....   = $ ....

    (Base Daily Budget)   (Yesterday's Leftover Balance)   (Today's Daily Budget)

Day 134		
Flexible Expense Name	**Category**	**Today's Daily Budget:** $ _____
		- $
		- $
		- $
		- $
		- $
		- $
		- $
		- $
	Leftover Balance	**= $**

$ ....   + $ ....   = $ ....

  (Base Daily Budget)   (Yesterday's Leftover Balance)   (Today's Daily Budget)

Day 135		
Flexible Expense Name	**Category**	**Today's Daily Budget:** $ _____
		- $
		- $
		- $
		- $
		- $
		- $
		- $
		- $
	Leftover Balance	**= $**

$ _____ + $ _____ = $ _____
(Base Daily Budget) (Yesterday's Leftover Balance) (Today's Daily Budget)

Day 136		
Flexible Expense Name	**Category**	**Today's Daily Budget:** $ _____
		– $
		– $
		– $
		– $
		– $
		– $
		– $
		– $
	Leftover Balance	**= $**

$ _____ + $ _____ = $ _____
(Base Daily Budget) (Yesterday's Leftover Balance) (Today's Daily Budget)

Day 137		
Flexible Expense Name	**Category**	**Today's Daily Budget:** $ _____
		– $
		– $
		– $
		– $
		– $
		– $
		– $
		– $
	Leftover Balance	**= $**

$ .... + $ .... = $ ....
(Base Daily Budget)   (Yesterday's Leftover Balance)   (Today's Daily Budget)

Day 138		
Flexible Expense Name	**Category**	**Today's Daily Budget:** $ _____
		- $
		- $
		- $
		- $
		- $
		- $
		- $
		- $
	Leftover Balance	**= $**

Weekly Reconciliation	
Flexible Expense Category	**This Week's Spend**
Groceries	$
Household Necessities	$
Self-Care/Wellness	$
Entertainment	$
Outside Food/Drink	$
Other Indulgences	$
Other Transportation	$
Other	$
Total Weekly Spend	$

$ .... + $ .... = $ ....
(Base Daily Budget)   (Yesterday's Leftover Balance)   (Today's Daily Budget)

Day 139		
Flexible Expense Name	**Category**	**Today's Daily Budget:** $ _____
		- $
		- $
		- $
		- $
		- $
		- $
		- $
		- $
	Leftover Balance	= $

$ .... + $ .... = $ ....
(Base Daily Budget)   (Yesterday's Leftover Balance)   (Today's Daily Budget)

Day 140		
Flexible Expense Name	**Category**	**Today's Daily Budget:** $ _____
		- $
		- $
		- $
		- $
		- $
		- $
		- $
		- $
	Leftover Balance	= $

$ .... + $ .... = $ ....
(Base Daily Budget)   (Yesterday's Leftover Balance)   (Today's Daily Budget)

Day 141		
Flexible Expense Name	**Category**	**Today's Daily Budget:** $ _____
		- $
		- $
		- $
		- $
		- $
		- $
		- $
	Leftover Balance	= $

$ .... + $ .... = $ ....
(Base Daily Budget)   (Yesterday's Leftover Balance)   (Today's Daily Budget)

Day 142		
Flexible Expense Name	**Category**	**Today's Daily Budget:** $ _____
		- $
		- $
		- $
		- $
		- $
		- $
		- $
		- $
	Leftover Balance	= $

$ .... + $ .... = $ ....
(Base Daily Budget)   (Yesterday's Leftover Balance)   (Today's Daily Budget)

Day 143		
Flexible Expense Name	**Category**	**Today's Daily Budget:** $ _____
		- $
		- $
		- $
		- $
		- $
		- $
		- $
		- $
	Leftover Balance	= $

$ .... + $ .... = $ ....
(Base Daily Budget)   (Yesterday's Leftover Balance)   (Today's Daily Budget)

Day 144		
Flexible Expense Name	**Category**	**Today's Daily Budget:** $ _____
		- $
		- $
		- $
		- $
		- $
		- $
		- $
		- $
	Leftover Balance	= $

$ .... + $ .... = $ ....

(Base Daily Budget)   (Yesterday's Leftover Balance)   (Today's Daily Budget)

Day 145

Flexible Expense Name	Category	Today's Daily Budget: $ _____
		- $
		- $
		- $
		- $
		- $
		- $
		- $
		- $
	Leftover Balance	= $

Weekly Reconciliation

Flexible Expense Category	This Week's Spend
Groceries	$
Household Necessities	$
Self-Care/Wellness	$
Entertainment	$
Outside Food/Drink	$
Other Indulgences	$
Other Transportation	$
Other	$
Total Weekly Spend	$

$ .... + $ .... = $ ....
(Base Daily Budget)   (Yesterday's Leftover Balance)   (Today's Daily Budget)

Day 146		
Flexible Expense Name	**Category**	**Today's Daily Budget:** $ _____
		− $
		− $
		− $
		− $
		− $
		− $
		− $
		− $
	Leftover Balance	**= $**

$ .... + $ .... = $ ....
(Base Daily Budget)   (Yesterday's Leftover Balance)   (Today's Daily Budget)

Day 147		
Flexible Expense Name	**Category**	**Today's Daily Budget:** $ _____
		− $
		− $
		− $
		− $
		− $
		− $
		− $
		− $
	Leftover Balance	**= $**

$ .... + $ .... = $ ....
(Base Daily Budget)   (Yesterday's Leftover Balance)   (Today's Daily Budget)

Day 148		
Flexible Expense Name	**Category**	**Today's Daily Budget:** $ _____
		- $
		- $
		- $
		- $
		- $
		- $
		- $
		- $
	Leftover Balance	= $

$ .... + $ .... = $ ....
(Base Daily Budget)   (Yesterday's Leftover Balance)   (Today's Daily Budget)

Day 149		
Flexible Expense Name	**Category**	**Today's Daily Budget:** $ _____
		- $
		- $
		- $
		- $
		- $
		- $
		- $
		- $
	Leftover Balance	= $

$ .... + $ .... = $ ....
(Base Daily Budget)   (Yesterday's Leftover Balance)   (Today's Daily Budget)

Day 150		
Flexible Expense Name	**Category**	**Today's Daily Budget:** $ _____
		- $
		- $
		- $
		- $
		- $
		- $
		- $
		- $
	Leftover Balance	= $

$ .... + $ .... = $ ....
(Base Daily Budget)   (Yesterday's Leftover Balance)   (Today's Daily Budget)

Day 151		
Flexible Expense Name	**Category**	**Today's Daily Budget:** $ _____
		- $
		- $
		- $
		- $
		- $
		- $
		- $
		- $
	Leftover Balance	= $

$ .... + $ .... = $ ....
(Base Daily Budget)   (Yesterday's Leftover Balance)   (Today's Daily Budget)

Day 152		
Flexible Expense Name	**Category**	**Today's Daily Budget:** $ _____
		- $
		- $
		- $
		- $
		- $
		- $
		- $
		- $
	Leftover Balance	**= $**

Weekly Reconciliation	
Flexible Expense Category	**This Week's Spend**
Groceries	$
Household Necessities	$
Self-Care/Wellness	$
Entertainment	$
Outside Food/Drink	$
Other Indulgences	$
Other Transportation	$
Other	$
Total Weekly Spend	$

$ .... + $ .... = $ ....
(Base Daily Budget)   (Yesterday's Leftover Balance)   (Today's Daily Budget)

Day 153		
Flexible Expense Name	**Category**	**Today's Daily Budget:** $ _____
		- $
		- $
		- $
		- $
		- $
		- $
		- $
		- $
	Leftover Balance	**= $**

$ .... + $ .... = $ ....
(Base Daily Budget)   (Yesterday's Leftover Balance)   (Today's Daily Budget)

Day 154		
Flexible Expense Name	**Category**	**Today's Daily Budget:** $ _____
		- $
		- $
		- $
		- $
		- $
		- $
		- $
		- $
	Leftover Balance	**= $**

$ .... + $ .... = $ ....

(Base Daily Budget)   (Yesterday's Leftover Balance)   (Today's Daily Budget)

Day 155		
Flexible Expense Name	**Category**	**Today's Daily Budget:** $ _____
		- $
		- $
		- $
		- $
		- $
		- $
		- $
		- $
	Leftover Balance	**= $**

Weekly Reconciliation	
Flexible Expense Category	**This Week's Spend**
Groceries	$
Household Necessities	$
Self-Care/Wellness	$
Entertainment	$
Outside Food/Drink	$
Other Indulgences	$
Other Transportation	$
Other	$
Total Weekly Spend	$

Month 5

Done.

Recapping Last Month

Monthly Reconciliation: <u>**Income**</u>		
Income Category	**Last Month's Forecasted Income**	**Last Month's Actual Income**
Total Active Income	$	$
Total Passive Income	$	$
Any Other Income	$	$
Total Monthly Income	$	$

(You can easily get your "Actual Amount Spent Last Month" values by summing up the "Total Weekly Spend" values in your weekly reconciliations)

Monthly Reconciliation: <u>**Flexible Expenses**</u>		
Flexible Expense Category	**Last Month's Budget**	**Actual Amount Spent Last Month**
Groceries	$	$
Household Necessities	$	$
Self-Care/Wellness	$	$
Entertainment	$	$
Outside Food/Drink	$	$
Other Indulgences	$	$
Other Transportation	$	$
Other	$	$
Total Monthly Flexible Expenses	$	$

Monthly Reconciliation: **Fixed Expenses**

Fixed Expense Category	Last Month's Budget	Actual Amount Spent Last Month
Rent/Mortgage	$	$
Bills	$	$
Car Payments	$	$
Insurance	$	$
Subscriptions	$	$
Other	$	$
Total Monthly Fixed Expenses	$	$

Monthly Reconciliation: **Debt Balance**

Debt Name	Beginning of Last Month Balance	Amount Budgeted For Last Month	Actual Amount Paid Last Month	Remaining Debt Balance
	$	$	$	$
	$	$	$	$
	$	$	$	$
	$	$	$	$
	$	$	$	$
	$	$	$	$
	$	$	$	$
	$	$	$	$
	$	$	$	$
	$	$	$	$
Debt Totals	$	$	$	$

Recap Questions

1. What did I overspend on unnecessarily this month?
   Why do I think that happened?

....

....

....

2. What adjustments do I need to make to my spending
   to set my future self up in a much better position?

....

....

....

3. What emotional impulses am I letting lead my spending habits?
   If I had ultimate willpower, what would I change in regards
   to my spending?

....

....

....

4. What have I learned about myself in relation to money? What
   specific actions can I take to improve based on what I've learned?

....

....

....

Month 6
Days
156 - 186

Monthly Budget Preparation

My main financial goal for the month:

This Month's Forecast: __Income__

Income Category	Forecasted Amount
Total Active Income	$
Total Passive Income	$
Any Other Income	$
This Month's Forecasted Income	$

This Month's Budget: __Fixed Expenses__

Fixed Expense Category	Budget
Rent/Mortgage	$
Bills	$
Car Payments	$
Insurance	$
Subscriptions	$
Other	$
This Month's Fixed Expense Budget	$

__Debt Clearing Planner__

Debt Name	Total Balance Remaining	Budget	Total Month's Remaining to Complete
	$	$	
	$	$	
	$	$	
	$	$	
	$	$	
	$	$	
	$	$	
	$	$	
	$	$	
	$	$	
This Month's Debt Budget			

$ _____   − $ _____   − $ _____

(This Month's
Forecasted Income)

(This Month's
Fixed Expense Budget)

(This Month's
Debt Budget)

= $ _____

(This Month's
Remaining Balance)

1. Now, choose how to allocate this remaining balance based on your personalized goals.

Note: These two fields' totals should add up to "This Month's Remaining Balance."

$ _____ $ _____

(This Month's
Savings Goal)

(This Month's Flexible
Expense Budget)

2. Next, take "This Month's Flexible Expense Budget" and break it down based on the following categories:

This Month's Budget: **Flexible Expenses**	
Flexible Expense Category	**This Month's Budget**
Groceries	$
Household Necessities	$
Self-Care/Wellness	$
Entertainment	$
Outside Food/Drink	$
Other Indulgences	$
Other Transportation	$
Other	$
This Month's Flexible Expense Budget	$

3. Lastly, we'll calculate the daily budget you need to adhere to in order to achieve your monthly budgeting goal:

$ _____   ÷   _____   = $ _____

(This Month's Flexible
Expense Budget)

(Total Days In
Upcoming Month)

(Base Daily Budget)

_____ , 20 ___
(Month)   (Year)

(This is an optional tool you can use to help get a visual overview of your entire month)

Mon	Tue	Wed	Thu	Fri	Sat	Sun

$ .... + $ .... = $ ....
(Base Daily Budget)   (Yesterday's Leftover Balance)   (Today's Daily Budget)

Day 156		
Flexible Expense Name	**Category**	**Today's Daily Budget:** $ _____
		- $
		- $
		- $
		- $
		- $
		- $
		- $
		- $
	Leftover Balance	**= $**

$ .... + $ .... = $ ....
(Base Daily Budget)   (Yesterday's Leftover Balance)   (Today's Daily Budget)

Day 157		
Flexible Expense Name	**Category**	**Today's Daily Budget:** $ _____
		- $
		- $
		- $
		- $
		- $
		- $
		- $
		- $
	Leftover Balance	**= $**

$ .... + $ .... = $ ....
(Base Daily Budget)   (Yesterday's Leftover Balance)   (Today's Daily Budget)

Day 158		
Flexible Expense Name	**Category**	**Today's Daily Budget:** $ _____
		- $
		- $
		- $
		- $
		- $
		- $
		- $
		- $
	Leftover Balance	**= $**

$ .... + $ .... = $ ....
(Base Daily Budget)   (Yesterday's Leftover Balance)   (Today's Daily Budget)

Day 159		
Flexible Expense Name	**Category**	**Today's Daily Budget:** $ _____
		- $
		- $
		- $
		- $
		- $
		- $
		- $
		- $
	Leftover Balance	**= $**

$ .... + $ .... = $ ....
(Base Daily Budget)   (Yesterday's Leftover Balance)   (Today's Daily Budget)

Day 160		
Flexible Expense Name	**Category**	**Today's Daily Budget:** $ _____
		- $
		- $
		- $
		- $
		- $
		- $
		- $
		- $
	Leftover Balance	**= $**

$ .... + $ .... = $ ....
(Base Daily Budget)   (Yesterday's Leftover Balance)   (Today's Daily Budget)

Day 161		
Flexible Expense Name	**Category**	**Today's Daily Budget:** $ _____
		- $
		- $
		- $
		- $
		- $
		- $
		- $
		- $
	Leftover Balance	**= $**

$ .... + $ .... = $ ....
(Base Daily Budget)   (Yesterday's Leftover Balance)   (Today's Daily Budget)

Day 162		
Flexible Expense Name	**Category**	**Today's Daily Budget:** $ _____
		- $
		- $
		- $
		- $
		- $
		- $
		- $
		- $
	Leftover Balance	**= $**

Weekly Reconciliation	
Flexible Expense Category	**This Week's Spend**
Groceries	$
Household Necessities	$
Self-Care/Wellness	$
Entertainment	$
Outside Food/Drink	$
Other Indulgences	$
Other Transportation	$
Other	$
Total Weekly Spend	$

$ .... + $ .... = $ ....
(Base Daily Budget)   (Yesterday's Leftover Balance)   (Today's Daily Budget)

Day 163		
Flexible Expense Name	**Category**	**Today's Daily Budget:** $ _____
		- $
		- $
		- $
		- $
		- $
		- $
		- $
		- $
	Leftover Balance	**= $**

$ .... + $ .... = $ ....
(Base Daily Budget)   (Yesterday's Leftover Balance)   (Today's Daily Budget)

Day 164		
Flexible Expense Name	**Category**	**Today's Daily Budget:** $ _____
		- $
		- $
		- $
		- $
		- $
		- $
		- $
		- $
	Leftover Balance	**= $**

$ .... + $ .... = $ ....

Day 165		
Flexible Expense Name	**Category**	**Today's Daily Budget:** $ _____
		- $
		- $
		- $
		- $
		- $
		- $
		- $
		- $
	Leftover Balance	= $

$ .... + $ .... = $ ....

Day 166		
Flexible Expense Name	**Category**	**Today's Daily Budget:** $ _____
		- $
		- $
		- $
		- $
		- $
		- $
		- $
		- $
	Leftover Balance	= $

$ .... + $ .... = $ ....
(Base Daily Budget)   (Yesterday's Leftover Balance)   (Today's Daily Budget)

Day 167		
Flexible Expense Name	**Category**	**Today's Daily Budget:** $ _____
		- $
		- $
		- $
		- $
		- $
		- $
		- $
		- $
	Leftover Balance	= $

$ .... + $ .... = $ ....
(Base Daily Budget)   (Yesterday's Leftover Balance)   (Today's Daily Budget)

Day 168		
Flexible Expense Name	**Category**	**Today's Daily Budget:** $ _____
		- $
		- $
		- $
		- $
		- $
		- $
		- $
		- $
	Leftover Balance	= $

$ _____ + $ _____ = $ _____
(Base Daily Budget)   (Yesterday's Leftover Balance)   (Today's Daily Budget)

Day 169		
Flexible Expense Name	**Category**	**Today's Daily Budget:** $ _____
		- $
		- $
		- $
		- $
		- $
		- $
		- $
		- $
	Leftover Balance	= $

Weekly Reconciliation	
Flexible Expense Category	**This Week's Spend**
Groceries	$
Household Necessities	$
Self-Care/Wellness	$
Entertainment	$
Outside Food/Drink	$
Other Indulgences	$
Other Transportation	$
Other	$
Total Weekly Spend	$

$ .... + $ .... = $ ....
(Base Daily Budget)   (Yesterday's Leftover Balance)   (Today's Daily Budget)

Day 170		
Flexible Expense Name	**Category**	**Today's Daily Budget:** $ _____
		- $
		- $
		- $
		- $
		- $
		- $
		- $
		- $
	Leftover Balance	= $

$ .... + $ .... = $ ....
(Base Daily Budget)   (Yesterday's Leftover Balance)   (Today's Daily Budget)

Day 171		
Flexible Expense Name	**Category**	**Today's Daily Budget:** $ _____
		- $
		- $
		- $
		- $
		- $
		- $
		- $
		- $
	Leftover Balance	= $

$ .... + $ .... = $ ....
(Base Daily Budget)   (Yesterday's Leftover Balance)   (Today's Daily Budget)

Day 172		
Flexible Expense Name	**Category**	**Today's Daily Budget:** $ _____
		- $
		- $
		- $
		- $
		- $
		- $
		- $
		- $
	Leftover Balance	**= $**

$ .... + $ .... = $ ....
(Base Daily Budget)   (Yesterday's Leftover Balance)   (Today's Daily Budget)

Day 173		
Flexible Expense Name	**Category**	**Today's Daily Budget:** $ _____
		- $
		- $
		- $
		- $
		- $
		- $
		- $
		- $
	Leftover Balance	**= $**

$ .... + $ .... = $ ....
(Base Daily Budget)   (Yesterday's Leftover Balance)   (Today's Daily Budget)

Day 174		
Flexible Expense Name	**Category**	**Today's Daily Budget:** $ _____
		- $
		- $
		- $
		- $
		- $
		- $
		- $
		- $
	Leftover Balance	**= $**

$ .... + $ .... = $ ....
(Base Daily Budget)   (Yesterday's Leftover Balance)   (Today's Daily Budget)

Day 175		
Flexible Expense Name	**Category**	**Today's Daily Budget:** $ _____
		- $
		- $
		- $
		- $
		- $
		- $
		- $
		- $
	Leftover Balance	**= $**

$ .... $\quad+\quad$ $ .... $\quad=\quad$ $ ....

(Base Daily Budget)   (Yesterday's Leftover Balance)   (Today's Daily Budget)

Day 176		
Flexible Expense Name	**Category**	**Today's Daily Budget:** $ _____
		- $
		- $
		- $
		- $
		- $
		- $
		- $
		- $
	Leftover Balance	**= $**

Weekly Reconciliation	
Flexible Expense Category	**This Week's Spend**
Groceries	$
Household Necessities	$
Self-Care/Wellness	$
Entertainment	$
Outside Food/Drink	$
Other Indulgences	$
Other Transportation	$
Other	$
Total Weekly Spend	$

$ .... $ + $ .... $ = $ ....
(Base Daily Budget)   (Yesterday's Leftover Balance)   (Today's Daily Budget)

Day 177		
Flexible Expense Name	Category	Today's Daily Budget: $ _____
		- $
		- $
		- $
		- $
		- $
		- $
		- $
		- $
	Leftover Balance	= $

$ .... $ + $ .... $ = $ ....
(Base Daily Budget)   (Yesterday's Leftover Balance)   (Today's Daily Budget)

Day 178		
Flexible Expense Name	Category	Today's Daily Budget: $ _____
		- $
		- $
		- $
		- $
		- $
		- $
		- $
		- $
	Leftover Balance	= $

$ .... + $ .... = $ ....

(Base Daily Budget)   *(Yesterday's Leftover Balance)*   *(Today's Daily Budget)*

Day 179		
Flexible Expense Name	**Category**	**Today's Daily Budget:** $ _____
		- $
		- $
		- $
		- $
		- $
		- $
		- $
		- $
	Leftover Balance	= $

$ .... + $ .... = $ ....

(Base Daily Budget)   *(Yesterday's Leftover Balance)*   *(Today's Daily Budget)*

Day 180		
Flexible Expense Name	**Category**	**Today's Daily Budget:** $ _____
		- $
		- $
		- $
		- $
		- $
		- $
		- $
		- $
	Leftover Balance	= $

$ .... + $ .... = $ ....
(Base Daily Budget)   (Yesterday's Leftover Balance)   (Today's Daily Budget)

Day 181		
Flexible Expense Name	**Category**	**Today's Daily Budget:** $\$$ _____
		- $
		- $
		- $
		- $
		- $
		- $
		- $
		- $
	Leftover Balance	= $

$ .... + $ .... = $ ....
(Base Daily Budget)   (Yesterday's Leftover Balance)   (Today's Daily Budget)

Day 182		
Flexible Expense Name	**Category**	**Today's Daily Budget:** $\$$ _____
		- $
		- $
		- $
		- $
		- $
		- $
		- $
		- $
	Leftover Balance	= $

$ .... + $ .... = $ ....
(Base Daily Budget)   (Yesterday's Leftover Balance)   (Today's Daily Budget)

Day 183		
Flexible Expense Name	**Category**	**Today's Daily Budget:** $ _____
		- $
		- $
		- $
		- $
		- $
		- $
		- $
		- $
	Leftover Balance	= $

Weekly Reconciliation	
Flexible Expense Category	**This Week's Spend**
Groceries	$
Household Necessities	$
Self-Care/Wellness	$
Entertainment	$
Outside Food/Drink	$
Other Indulgences	$
Other Transportation	$
Other	$
Total Weekly Spend	$

$ .... + $ .... = $ ....
(Base Daily Budget)   (Yesterday's Leftover Balance)   (Today's Daily Budget)

Day 184		
Flexible Expense Name	**Category**	**Today's Daily Budget:** $ _____
		- $
		- $
		- $
		- $
		- $
		- $
		- $
	Leftover Balance	**= $**

$ .... + $ .... = $ ....
(Base Daily Budget)   (Yesterday's Leftover Balance)   (Today's Daily Budget)

Day 185		
Flexible Expense Name	**Category**	**Today's Daily Budget:** $ _____
		- $
		- $
		- $
		- $
		- $
		- $
		- $
		- $
	Leftover Balance	**= $**

$ ....
(Base Daily Budget)

+ $ ....
(Yesterday's Leftover Balance)

= $ ....
(Today's Daily Budget)

Day 186		
Flexible Expense Name	**Category**	**Today's Daily Budget:** $ _____
		- $
		- $
		- $
		- $
		- $
		- $
		- $
		- $
	Leftover Balance	**= $**

Weekly Reconciliation	
Flexible Expense Category	**This Week's Spend**
Groceries	$
Household Necessities	$
Self-Care/Wellness	$
Entertainment	$
Outside Food/Drink	$
Other Indulgences	$
Other Transportation	$
Other	$
Total Weekly Spend	$

Month 6

Done.

Recapping Last Month

Income Category	Last Month's Forecasted Income	Last Month's Actual Income
Total Active Income	$	$
Total Passive Income	$	$
Any Other Income	$	$
Total Monthly Income	$	$

(You can easily get your "Actual Amount Spent Last Month" values by summing up the "Total Weekly Spend" values in your weekly reconciliations)

Monthly Reconciliation: **Flexible Expenses**

Flexible Expense Category	Last Month's Budget	Actual Amount Spent Last Month
Groceries	$	$
Household Necessities	$	$
Self-Care/Wellness	$	$
Entertainment	$	$
Outside Food/Drink	$	$
Other Indulgences	$	$
Other Transportation	$	$
Other	$	$
Total Monthly Flexible Expenses	$	$

Monthly Reconciliation: **Fixed Expenses**

Fixed Expense Category	Last Month's Budget	Actual Amount Spent Last Month
Rent/Mortgage	$	$
Bills	$	$
Car Payments	$	$
Insurance	$	$
Subscriptions	$	$
Other	$	$
Total Monthly Fixed Expenses	$	$

Monthly Reconciliation: **Debt Balance**

Debt Name	Beginning of Last Month Balance	Amount Budgeted For Last Month	Actual Amount Paid Last Month	Remaining Debt Balance
	$	$	$	$
	$	$	$	$
	$	$	$	$
	$	$	$	$
	$	$	$	$
	$	$	$	$
	$	$	$	$
	$	$	$	$
	$	$	$	$
	$	$	$	$
Debt Totals	$	$	$	$

Recap Questions

1. What did I overspend on unnecessarily this month?
   Why do I think that happened?

....

....

....

2. What adjustments do I need to make to my spending
   to set my future self up in a much better position?

....

....

....

3. What will I tell myself if I spend over my daily budget one day?
   What actions will I take the following day(s) to get back on track?

....

....

....

4. In what ways can I be more supportive and forgiving of
   myself on this journey? How am I being too hard on myself?

....

....

....

Month 7

Days 187 - 217

Monthly Budget Preparation

My main financial goal for the month:

This Month's Forecast: __Income__

Income Category	Forecasted Amount
Total Active Income	$
Total Passive Income	$
Any Other Income	$
This Month's Forecasted Income	$

This Month's Budget: __Fixed Expenses__

Fixed Expense Category	Budget
Rent/Mortgage	$
Bills	$
Car Payments	$
Insurance	$
Subscriptions	$
Other	$
This Month's Fixed Expense Budget	$

Debt Clearing Planner

Debt Name	Total Balance Remaining	Budget	Total Month's Remaining to Complete
	$	$	
	$	$	
	$	$	
	$	$	
	$	$	
	$	$	
	$	$	
	$	$	
	$	$	
	$	$	
This Month's Debt Budget			

$ .... – $ .... – $ ....

(This Month's
Forecasted Income)

(This Month's
Fixed Expense Budget)

(This Month's
Debt Budget)

= $ ....

1. **Now, choose how to allocate this remaining balance based on your personalized goals.**

(This Month's
Remaining Balance)

Note: These two fields' totals should add up to "This Month's Remaining Balance."

$ ....

$ ....

(This Month's
Savings Goal)

(This Month's Flexible
Expense Budget)

2. **Next, take "This Month's Flexible Expense Budget" and break it down based on the following categories:**

This Month's Budget: **Flexible Expenses**	
Flexible Expense Category	**This Month's Budget**
Groceries	$
Household Necessities	$
Self-Care/Wellness	$
Entertainment	$
Outside Food/Drink	$
Other Indulgences	$
Other Transportation	$
Other	$
This Month's Flexible Expense Budget	$

3. **Lastly, we'll calculate the daily budget you need to adhere to in order to achieve your monthly budgeting goal:**

$ .... ÷ .... = $ ....

(This Month's Flexible
Expense Budget)

(Total Days In
Upcoming Month)

(Base Daily Budget)

_____ , 20 ___

(Month)   (Year)

(This is an optional tool you can use to help get a visual overview of your entire month)

Mon	Tue	Wed	Thu	Fri	Sat	Sun

$ .... + $ .... = $ ....
(Base Daily Budget)   (Yesterday's Leftover Balance)   (Today's Daily Budget)

Day 187		
Flexible Expense Name	**Category**	**Today's Daily Budget:** $ _____
		- $
		- $
		- $
		- $
		- $
		- $
		- $
		- $
	Leftover Balance	= $

$ .... + $ .... = $ ....
(Base Daily Budget)   (Yesterday's Leftover Balance)   (Today's Daily Budget)

Day 188		
Flexible Expense Name	**Category**	**Today's Daily Budget:** $ _____
		- $
		- $
		- $
		- $
		- $
		- $
		- $
		- $
	Leftover Balance	= $

$ .... + $ .... = $ ....
(Base Daily Budget)   (Yesterday's Leftover Balance)   (Today's Daily Budget)

Day 189		
Flexible Expense Name	**Category**	**Today's Daily Budget:** $ _____
		- $
		- $
		- $
		- $
		- $
		- $
		- $
		- $
	Leftover Balance	**= $**

$ .... + $ .... = $ ....
(Base Daily Budget)   (Yesterday's Leftover Balance)   (Today's Daily Budget)

Day 190		
Flexible Expense Name	**Category**	**Today's Daily Budget:** $ _____
		- $
		- $
		- $
		- $
		- $
		- $
		- $
		- $
	Leftover Balance	**= $**

$ .... + $ .... = $ ....
(Base Daily Budget)   (Yesterday's Leftover Balance)   (Today's Daily Budget)

Day 191		
Flexible Expense Name	**Category**	**Today's Daily Budget:** $ _____
		- $
		- $
		- $
		- $
		- $
		- $
		- $
		- $
	Leftover Balance	**= $**

$ .... + $ .... = $ ....
(Base Daily Budget)   (Yesterday's Leftover Balance)   (Today's Daily Budget)

Day 192		
Flexible Expense Name	**Category**	**Today's Daily Budget:** $ _____
		- $
		- $
		- $
		- $
		- $
		- $
		- $
		- $
	Leftover Balance	**= $**

$ _____ + $ _____ = $ _____

(Base Daily Budget)   (Yesterday's Leftover Balance)   (Today's Daily Budget)

Day 193		
Flexible Expense Name	**Category**	**Today's Daily Budget:** $ _____
		- $
		- $
		- $
		- $
		- $
		- $
		- $
		- $
	Leftover Balance	= $

Weekly Reconciliation	
Flexible Expense Category	**This Week's Spend**
Groceries	$
Household Necessities	$
Self-Care/Wellness	$
Entertainment	$
Outside Food/Drink	$
Other Indulgences	$
Other Transportation	$
Other	$
Total Weekly Spend	$

$ .... + $ .... = $ ....
(Base Daily Budget)   (Yesterday's Leftover Balance)   (Today's Daily Budget)

Day 194		
Flexible Expense Name	**Category**	**Today's Daily Budget:** $ _____
		- $
		- $
		- $
		- $
		- $
		- $
		- $
		- $
	Leftover Balance	= $

$ .... + $ .... = $ ....
(Base Daily Budget)   (Yesterday's Leftover Balance)   (Today's Daily Budget)

Day 195		
Flexible Expense Name	**Category**	**Today's Daily Budget:** $ _____
		- $
		- $
		- $
		- $
		- $
		- $
		- $
		- $
	Leftover Balance	= $

$ .... + $ .... = $ ....
(Base Daily Budget)   (Yesterday's Leftover Balance)   (Today's Daily Budget)

Day 196		
Flexible Expense Name	**Category**	**Today's Daily Budget:** $ _____
		- $
		- $
		- $
		- $
		- $
		- $
		- $
	Leftover Balance	**= $**

$ .... + $ .... = $ ....
(Base Daily Budget)   (Yesterday's Leftover Balance)   (Today's Daily Budget)

Day 197		
Flexible Expense Name	**Category**	**Today's Daily Budget:** $ _____
		- $
		- $
		- $
		- $
		- $
		- $
		- $
		- $
	Leftover Balance	**= $**

$ .... + $ .... = $ ....
(Base Daily Budget)   (Yesterday's Leftover Balance)   (Today's Daily Budget)

Day 198		
Flexible Expense Name	**Category**	**Today's Daily Budget:** $ _____
		- $
		- $
		- $
		- $
		- $
		- $
		- $
		- $
	Leftover Balance	**= $**

$ .... + $ .... = $ ....
(Base Daily Budget)   (Yesterday's Leftover Balance)   (Today's Daily Budget)

Day 199		
Flexible Expense Name	**Category**	**Today's Daily Budget:** $ _____
		- $
		- $
		- $
		- $
		- $
		- $
		- $
		- $
	Leftover Balance	**= $**

$ .... + $ .... = $ ....
(Base Daily Budget)   (Yesterday's Leftover Balance)   (Today's Daily Budget)

Day 200		
Flexible Expense Name	**Category**	**Today's Daily Budget:** $ _____
		- $
		- $
		- $
		- $
		- $
		- $
		- $
		- $
	Leftover Balance	**= $**

Weekly Reconciliation	
Flexible Expense Category	**This Week's Spend**
Groceries	$
Household Necessities	$
Self-Care/Wellness	$
Entertainment	$
Outside Food/Drink	$
Other Indulgences	$
Other Transportation	$
Other	$
Total Weekly Spend	$

$ .... + $ .... = $ ....
(Base Daily Budget)   (Yesterday's Leftover Balance)   (Today's Daily Budget)

Day 201		
Flexible Expense Name	**Category**	**Today's Daily Budget:** $ _____
		- $
		- $
		- $
		- $
		- $
		- $
		- $
		- $
	Leftover Balance	= $

$ .... + $ .... = $ ....
(Base Daily Budget)   (Yesterday's Leftover Balance)   (Today's Daily Budget)

Day 202		
Flexible Expense Name	**Category**	**Today's Daily Budget:** $ _____
		- $
		- $
		- $
		- $
		- $
		- $
		- $
		- $
	Leftover Balance	= $

$ .... + $ .... = $ ....
(Base Daily Budget)   (Yesterday's Leftover Balance)   (Today's Daily Budget)

Day 203		
Flexible Expense Name	**Category**	**Today's Daily Budget:** $ _____
		- $
		- $
		- $
		- $
		- $
		- $
		- $
		- $
	Leftover Balance	= $

$ .... + $ .... = $ ....
(Base Daily Budget)   (Yesterday's Leftover Balance)   (Today's Daily Budget)

Day 204		
Flexible Expense Name	**Category**	**Today's Daily Budget:** $ _____
		- $
		- $
		- $
		- $
		- $
		- $
		- $
		- $
	Leftover Balance	= $

$ .... + $ .... = $ ....
(Base Daily Budget)   (Yesterday's Leftover Balance)   (Today's Daily Budget)

Day 205		
Flexible Expense Name	**Category**	**Today's Daily Budget:** $ _____
		- $
		- $
		- $
		- $
		- $
		- $
		- $
		- $
	Leftover Balance	**= $**

$ .... + $ .... = $ ....
(Base Daily Budget)   (Yesterday's Leftover Balance)   (Today's Daily Budget)

Day 206		
Flexible Expense Name	**Category**	**Today's Daily Budget:** $ _____
		- $
		- $
		- $
		- $
		- $
		- $
		- $
		- $
	Leftover Balance	**= $**

$ .... + $ .... = $ ....

(Base Daily Budget)   (Yesterday's Leftover Balance)   (Today's Daily Budget)

Day 207		
Flexible Expense Name	**Category**	**Today's Daily Budget:** $ _____
		- $
		- $
		- $
		- $
		- $
		- $
		- $
		- $
	Leftover Balance	**= $**

Weekly Reconciliation	
Flexible Expense Category	**This Week's Spend**
Groceries	$
Household Necessities	$
Self-Care/Wellness	$
Entertainment	$
Outside Food/Drink	$
Other Indulgences	$
Other Transportation	$
Other	$
Total Weekly Spend	$

$ .... + $ .... = $ ....

(Base Daily Budget)   (Yesterday's Leftover Balance)   (Today's Daily Budget)

Day 208		
Flexible Expense Name	**Category**	**Today's Daily Budget:** $ _____
		- $
		- $
		- $
		- $
		- $
		- $
		- $
		- $
	Leftover Balance	= $

$ .... + $ .... = $ ....

(Base Daily Budget)   (Yesterday's Leftover Balance)   (Today's Daily Budget)

Day 209		
Flexible Expense Name	**Category**	**Today's Daily Budget:** $ _____
		- $
		- $
		- $
		- $
		- $
		- $
		- $
		- $
	Leftover Balance	= $

$ .... + $ .... = $ ....
(Base Daily Budget)   (Yesterday's Leftover Balance)   (Today's Daily Budget)

Day 210		
Flexible Expense Name	**Category**	**Today's Daily Budget:** $ _____
		- $
		- $
		- $
		- $
		- $
		- $
		- $
		- $
	Leftover Balance	**= $**

$ .... + $ .... = $ ....
(Base Daily Budget)   (Yesterday's Leftover Balance)   (Today's Daily Budget)

Day 211		
Flexible Expense Name	**Category**	**Today's Daily Budget:** $ _____
		- $
		- $
		- $
		- $
		- $
		- $
		- $
		- $
	Leftover Balance	**= $**

$ .... + $ .... = $ ....
(Base Daily Budget)   (Yesterday's Leftover Balance)   (Today's Daily Budget)

Day 212		
Flexible Expense Name	**Category**	**Today's Daily Budget:** $ _____
		- $
		- $
		- $
		- $
		- $
		- $
		- $
		- $
	Leftover Balance	**= $**

$ .... + $ .... = $ ....
(Base Daily Budget)   (Yesterday's Leftover Balance)   (Today's Daily Budget)

Day 213		
Flexible Expense Name	**Category**	**Today's Daily Budget:** $ _____
		- $
		- $
		- $
		- $
		- $
		- $
		- $
		- $
	Leftover Balance	**= $**

$ .... + $ .... = $ ....

(Base Daily Budget)   (Yesterday's Leftover Balance)   (Today's Daily Budget)

Day 214		
Flexible Expense Name	**Category**	**Today's Daily Budget:** $ _____
		- $
		- $
		- $
		- $
		- $
		- $
		- $
		- $
	Leftover Balance	= $

Weekly Reconciliation	
Flexible Expense Category	**This Week's Spend**
Groceries	$
Household Necessities	$
Self-Care/Wellness	$
Entertainment	$
Outside Food/Drink	$
Other Indulgences	$
Other Transportation	$
Other	$
Total Weekly Spend	$

$ .... + $ .... = $ ....
(Base Daily Budget)   (Yesterday's Leftover Balance)   (Today's Daily Budget)

Day 215		
Flexible Expense Name	**Category**	**Today's Daily Budget:** $ _____
		- $
		- $
		- $
		- $
		- $
		- $
		- $
		- $
	Leftover Balance	= $

$ .... + $ .... = $ ....
(Base Daily Budget)   (Yesterday's Leftover Balance)   (Today's Daily Budget)

Day 216		
Flexible Expense Name	**Category**	**Today's Daily Budget:** $ _____
		- $
		- $
		- $
		- $
		- $
		- $
		- $
		- $
	Leftover Balance	= $

$ .... (Base Daily Budget) + $ .... (Yesterday's Leftover Balance) = $ .... (Today's Daily Budget)

Day 217		
Flexible Expense Name	**Category**	**Today's Daily Budget:** $ _____
		- $
		- $
		- $
		- $
		- $
		- $
		- $
		- $
	Leftover Balance	**= $**

Weekly Reconciliation	
Flexible Expense Category	**This Week's Spend**
Groceries	$
Household Necessities	$
Self-Care/Wellness	$
Entertainment	$
Outside Food/Drink	$
Other Indulgences	$
Other Transportation	$
Other	$
Total Weekly Spend	$

Month 7

Done.

Recapping Last Month

Monthly Reconciliation: **Income**		
Income Category	**Last Month's Forecasted Income**	**Last Month's Actual Income**
Total Active Income	$	$
Total Passive Income	$	$
Any Other Income	$	$
Total Monthly Income	$	$

(You can easily get your "Actual Amount Spent Last Month" values by summing up the "Total Weekly Spend" values in your weekly reconciliations)

Monthly Reconciliation: **Flexible Expenses**		
Flexible Expense Category	**Last Month's Budget**	**Actual Amount Spent Last Month**
Groceries	$	$
Household Necessities	$	$
Self-Care/Wellness	$	$
Entertainment	$	$
Outside Food/Drink	$	$
Other Indulgences	$	$
Other Transportation	$	$
Other	$	$
Total Monthly Flexible Expenses	$	$

Monthly Reconciliation: **Fixed Expenses**

Fixed Expense Category	Last Month's Budget	Actual Amount Spent Last Month
Rent/Mortgage	$	$
Bills	$	$
Car Payments	$	$
Insurance	$	$
Subscriptions	$	$
Other	$	$
Total Monthly Fixed Expenses	$	$

Monthly Reconciliation: **Debt Balance**

Debt Name	Beginning of Last Month Balance	Amount Budgeted For Last Month	Actual Amount Paid Last Month	Remaining Debt Balance
	$	$	$	$
	$	$	$	$
	$	$	$	$
	$	$	$	$
	$	$	$	$
	$	$	$	$
	$	$	$	$
	$	$	$	$
	$	$	$	$
	$	$	$	$
Debt Totals	$	$	$	$

Recap Questions

1. What did I overspend on unnecessarily this month?
   Why do I think that happened?

....

....

....

2. What adjustments do I need to make to my spending
   to set my future self up in a much better position?

....

....

....

3. What will I tell myself if I spend over my daily budget one day?
   What actions will I take the following day(s) to get back on track?

....

....

....

4. In what ways can I be more supportive and forgiving of
   myself on this journey? How am I being too hard on myself?

....

....

....

Month 8
Days
218 - 248

Monthly Budget Preparation

My main financial goal for the month:

This Month's Forecast: **Income**

Income Category	Forecasted Amount
Total Active Income	$
Total Passive Income	$
Any Other Income	$
This Month's Forecasted Income	$

This Month's Budget: **Fixed Expenses**

Fixed Expense Category	Budget
Rent/Mortgage	$
Bills	$
Car Payments	$
Insurance	$
Subscriptions	$
Other	$
This Month's Fixed Expense Budget	$

Debt Clearing Planner

Debt Name	Total Balance Remaining	Budget	Total Month's Remaining to Complete
	$	$	
	$	$	
	$	$	
	$	$	
	$	$	
	$	$	
	$	$	
	$	$	
	$	$	
	$	$	
This Month's Debt Budget			

$ _____ − $ _____ − $ _____
(This Month's   (This Month's   (This Month's
Forecasted Income)   Fixed Expense Budget)   Debt Budget)

= $ _____

(This Month's
Remaining Balance)

1. Now, choose how to allocate this remaining balance based on your personalized goals.

Note: These two fields' totals should add up to "This Month's Remaining Balance."

$ _____ $ _____

(This Month's   (This Month's Flexible
Savings Goal)   Expense Budget)

2. Next, take "This Month's Flexible Expense Budget" and break it down based on the following categories:

This Month's Budget: **Flexible Expenses**	
Flexible Expense Category	**This Month's Budget**
Groceries	$
Household Necessities	$
Self-Care/Wellness	$
Entertainment	$
Outside Food/Drink	$
Other Indulgences	$
Other Transportation	$
Other	$
This Month's Flexible Expense Budget	$

3. Lastly, we'll calculate the daily budget you need to adhere to in order to achieve your monthly budgeting goal:

$ _____ ÷ _____ = $ _____

(This Month's Flexible   (Total Days In   (Base Daily Budget)
Expense Budget)   Upcoming Month)

_____ , 20 _____

(Month) (Year)

(This is an optional tool you can use to help get a visual overview of your entire month)

Mon	Tue	Wed	Thu	Fri	Sat	Sun

$ .... + $ .... = $ ....
(Base Daily Budget)   (Yesterday's Leftover Balance)   (Today's Daily Budget)

Day 218		
Flexible Expense Name	**Category**	**Today's Daily Budget:** $ _____
		- $
		- $
		- $
		- $
		- $
		- $
		- $
		- $
	Leftover Balance	= $

$ .... + $ .... = $ ....
(Base Daily Budget)   (Yesterday's Leftover Balance)   (Today's Daily Budget)

Day 219		
Flexible Expense Name	**Category**	**Today's Daily Budget:** $ _____
		- $
		- $
		- $
		- $
		- $
		- $
		- $
		- $
	Leftover Balance	= $

$ .... + $ .... = $ ....
(Base Daily Budget)   (Yesterday's Leftover Balance)   (Today's Daily Budget)

Day 220		
Flexible Expense Name	**Category**	**Today's Daily Budget:** $ _____
		- $
		- $
		- $
		- $
		- $
		- $
		- $
		- $
	Leftover Balance	= $

$ .... + $ .... = $ ....
(Base Daily Budget)   (Yesterday's Leftover Balance)   (Today's Daily Budget)

Day 221		
Flexible Expense Name	**Category**	**Today's Daily Budget:** $ _____
		- $
		- $
		- $
		- $
		- $
		- $
		- $
		- $
	Leftover Balance	= $

$ ....
(Base Daily Budget)

+ $ ....
(Yesterday's Leftover Balance)

= $ ....
(Today's Daily Budget)

Day 222		
Flexible Expense Name	**Category**	**Today's Daily Budget:** $ _____
		- $
		- $
		- $
		- $
		- $
		- $
		- $
		- $
	Leftover Balance	= $

$ ....
(Base Daily Budget)

+ $ ....
(Yesterday's Leftover Balance)

= $ ....
(Today's Daily Budget)

Day 223		
Flexible Expense Name	**Category**	**Today's Daily Budget:** $ _____
		- $
		- $
		- $
		- $
		- $
		- $
		- $
		- $
	Leftover Balance	= $

$ .... + $ .... = $ ....

(Base Daily Budget)   (Yesterday's Leftover Balance)   (Today's Daily Budget)

Day 224		
Flexible Expense Name	**Category**	**Today's Daily Budget:** $ _____
		- $
		- $
		- $
		- $
		- $
		- $
		- $
		- $
	Leftover Balance	**= $**

Weekly Reconciliation	
Flexible Expense Category	**This Week's Spend**
Groceries	$
Household Necessities	$
Self-Care/Wellness	$
Entertainment	$
Outside Food/Drink	$
Other Indulgences	$
Other Transportation	$
Other	$
Total Weekly Spend	$

$ ....   + $ ....   = $ ....

(Base Daily Budget)   (Yesterday's Leftover Balance)   (Today's Daily Budget)

Day 225		
Flexible Expense Name	**Category**	**Today's Daily Budget:** $ _____
		- $
		- $
		- $
		- $
		- $
		- $
		- $
		- $
	Leftover Balance	= $

$ ....   + $ ....   = $ ....

(Base Daily Budget)   (Yesterday's Leftover Balance)   (Today's Daily Budget)

Day 226		
Flexible Expense Name	**Category**	**Today's Daily Budget:** $ _____
		- $
		- $
		- $
		- $
		- $
		- $
		- $
		- $
	Leftover Balance	= $

$ .... + $ .... = $ ....

(Base Daily Budget)   (Yesterday's Leftover Balance)   (Today's Daily Budget)

Day 227		
Flexible Expense Name	**Category**	**Today's Daily Budget:** $ _____
		- $
		- $
		- $
		- $
		- $
		- $
		- $
		- $
	Leftover Balance	**= $**

$ .... + $ .... = $ ....

(Base Daily Budget)   (Yesterday's Leftover Balance)   (Today's Daily Budget)

Day 228		
Flexible Expense Name	**Category**	**Today's Daily Budget:** $ _____
		- $
		- $
		- $
		- $
		- $
		- $
		- $
		- $
	Leftover Balance	**= $**

$ .... + $ .... = $ ....

(Base Daily Budget)   (Yesterday's Leftover Balance)   (Today's Daily Budget)

Day 229		
Flexible Expense Name	**Category**	**Today's Daily Budget:** $ _____
		- $
		- $
		- $
		- $
		- $
		- $
		- $
		- $
	Leftover Balance	**= $**

$ .... + $ .... = $ ....

(Base Daily Budget)   (Yesterday's Leftover Balance)   (Today's Daily Budget)

Day 230		
Flexible Expense Name	**Category**	**Today's Daily Budget:** $ _____
		- $
		- $
		- $
		- $
		- $
		- $
		- $
		- $
	Leftover Balance	**= $**

$ .... + $ .... = $ ....
(Base Daily Budget)   (Yesterday's Leftover Balance)   (Today's Daily Budget)

Day 231		
Flexible Expense Name	**Category**	**Today's Daily Budget:** $ _____
		- $
		- $
		- $
		- $
		- $
		- $
		- $
		- $
	Leftover Balance	**= $**

Weekly Reconciliation	
Flexible Expense Category	**This Week's Spend**
Groceries	$
Household Necessities	$
Self-Care/Wellness	$
Entertainment	$
Outside Food/Drink	$
Other Indulgences	$
Other Transportation	$
Other	$
Total Weekly Spend	$

$ .... + $ .... = $ ....
(Base Daily Budget)   (Yesterday's Leftover Balance)   (Today's Daily Budget)

Day 232		
Flexible Expense Name	**Category**	**Today's Daily Budget:** $ _____
		- $
		- $
		- $
		- $
		- $
		- $
		- $
		- $
	Leftover Balance	= $

$ .... + $ .... = $ ....
(Base Daily Budget)   (Yesterday's Leftover Balance)   (Today's Daily Budget)

Day 233		
Flexible Expense Name	**Category**	**Today's Daily Budget:** $ _____
		- $
		- $
		- $
		- $
		- $
		- $
		- $
		- $
	Leftover Balance	= $

$ .... + $ .... = $ ....
(Base Daily Budget)   *(Yesterday's Leftover Balance)*   *(Today's Daily Budget)*

Day 234		
Flexible Expense Name	**Category**	**Today's Daily Budget:** $ _____
		- $
		- $
		- $
		- $
		- $
		- $
		- $
		- $
	Leftover Balance	= $

$ .... + $ .... = $ ....
(Base Daily Budget)   *(Yesterday's Leftover Balance)*   *(Today's Daily Budget)*

Day 235		
Flexible Expense Name	**Category**	**Today's Daily Budget:** $ _____
		- $
		- $
		- $
		- $
		- $
		- $
		- $
		- $
	Leftover Balance	= $

$ .... + $ .... = $ ....
(Base Daily Budget)   (Yesterday's Leftover Balance)   (Today's Daily Budget)

Day 236		
Flexible Expense Name	**Category**	**Today's Daily Budget:** $ _____
		- $
		- $
		- $
		- $
		- $
		- $
		- $
		- $
	Leftover Balance	= $

$ .... + $ .... = $ ....
(Base Daily Budget)   (Yesterday's Leftover Balance)   (Today's Daily Budget)

Day 237		
Flexible Expense Name	**Category**	**Today's Daily Budget:** $ _____
		- $
		- $
		- $
		- $
		- $
		- $
		- $
		- $
	Leftover Balance	= $

$ .... + $ .... = $ ....
(Base Daily Budget)   (Yesterday's Leftover Balance)   (Today's Daily Budget)

Day 238		
Flexible Expense Name	**Category**	**Today's Daily Budget:** $ _____
		- $
		- $
		- $
		- $
		- $
		- $
		- $
		- $
	Leftover Balance	**= $**

Weekly Reconciliation	
Flexible Expense Category	**This Week's Spend**
Groceries	$
Household Necessities	$
Self-Care/Wellness	$
Entertainment	$
Outside Food/Drink	$
Other Indulgences	$
Other Transportation	$
Other	$
Total Weekly Spend	$

$ .... + $ .... = $ ....
(Base Daily Budget)   (Yesterday's Leftover Balance)   (Today's Daily Budget)

Day 239		
Flexible Expense Name	**Category**	**Today's Daily Budget:** $ _____
		- $
		- $
		- $
		- $
		- $
		- $
		- $
		- $
	Leftover Balance	= $

$ .... + $ .... = $ ....
(Base Daily Budget)   (Yesterday's Leftover Balance)   (Today's Daily Budget)

Day 240		
Flexible Expense Name	**Category**	**Today's Daily Budget:** $ _____
		- $
		- $
		- $
		- $
		- $
		- $
		- $
		- $
	Leftover Balance	= $

$ .... + $ .... = $ ....
(Base Daily Budget)   (Yesterday's Leftover Balance)   (Today's Daily Budget)

Day 241		
Flexible Expense Name	**Category**	**Today's Daily Budget:** $ _____
		- $
		- $
		- $
		- $
		- $
		- $
		- $
		- $
	Leftover Balance	**= $**

$ .... + $ .... = $ ....
(Base Daily Budget)   (Yesterday's Leftover Balance)   (Today's Daily Budget)

Day 242		
Flexible Expense Name	**Category**	**Today's Daily Budget:** $ _____
		- $
		- $
		- $
		- $
		- $
		- $
		- $
		- $
	Leftover Balance	**= $**

$ .... + $ .... = $ ....
(Base Daily Budget)   (Yesterday's Leftover Balance)   (Today's Daily Budget)

Day 243		
Flexible Expense Name	**Category**	**Today's Daily Budget:** $ _____
		- $
		- $
		- $
		- $
		- $
		- $
		- $
		- $
	Leftover Balance	**= $**

$ .... + $ .... = $ ....
(Base Daily Budget)   (Yesterday's Leftover Balance)   (Today's Daily Budget)

Day 244		
Flexible Expense Name	**Category**	**Today's Daily Budget:** $ _____
		- $
		- $
		- $
		- $
		- $
		- $
		- $
		- $
	Leftover Balance	**= $**

$ .... + $ .... = $ ....

(Base Daily Budget)   (Yesterday's Leftover Balance)   (Today's Daily Budget)

Day 245		
Flexible Expense Name	**Category**	**Today's Daily Budget:** $ _____
		- $
		- $
		- $
		- $
		- $
		- $
		- $
		- $
	Leftover Balance	**= $**

Weekly Reconciliation	
Flexible Expense Category	**This Week's Spend**
Groceries	$
Household Necessities	$
Self-Care/Wellness	$
Entertainment	$
Outside Food/Drink	$
Other Indulgences	$
Other Transportation	$
Other	$
Total Weekly Spend	$

$ .... + $ .... = $ ....
  (Base Daily Budget)   (Yesterday's Leftover Balance)   (Today's Daily Budget)

Day 246		
Flexible Expense Name	**Category**	**Today's Daily Budget:** $\$$ _____
		- $
		- $
		- $
		- $
		- $
		- $
		- $
		- $
	Leftover Balance	**= $**

$ .... + $ .... = $ ....
  (Base Daily Budget)   (Yesterday's Leftover Balance)   (Today's Daily Budget)

Day 247		
Flexible Expense Name	**Category**	**Today's Daily Budget:** $\$$ _____
		- $
		- $
		- $
		- $
		- $
		- $
		- $
		- $
	Leftover Balance	**= $**

$ .... + $ .... = $ ....
(Base Daily Budget)   (Yesterday's Leftover Balance)   (Today's Daily Budget)

Day 248		
Flexible Expense Name	**Category**	**Today's Daily Budget:** $ _____
		- $
		- $
		- $
		- $
		- $
		- $
		- $
		- $
	Leftover Balance	**= $**

Weekly Reconciliation	
Flexible Expense Category	**This Week's Spend**
Groceries	$
Household Necessities	$
Self-Care/Wellness	$
Entertainment	$
Outside Food/Drink	$
Other Indulgences	$
Other Transportation	$
Other	$
Total Weekly Spend	$

Month 8

Done.

Recapping Last Month

Income Category	Last Month's Forecasted Income	Last Month's Actual Income
Total Active Income	$	$
Total Passive Income	$	$
Any Other Income	$	$
Total Monthly Income	$	$

(You can easily get your "Actual Amount Spent Last Month" values by summing up the "Total Weekly Spend" values in your weekly reconciliations)

Monthly Reconciliation: **Flexible Expenses**

Flexible Expense Category	Last Month's Budget	Actual Amount Spent Last Month
Groceries	$	$
Household Necessities	$	$
Self-Care/Wellness	$	$
Entertainment	$	$
Outside Food/Drink	$	$
Other Indulgences	$	$
Other Transportation	$	$
Other	$	$
Total Monthly Flexible Expenses	$	$

Monthly Reconciliation: **Fixed Expenses**

Fixed Expense Category	Last Month's Budget	Actual Amount Spent Last Month
Rent/Mortgage	$	$
Bills	$	$
Car Payments	$	$
Insurance	$	$
Subscriptions	$	$
Other	$	$
Total Monthly Fixed Expenses	$	$

Monthly Reconciliation: **Debt Balance**

Debt Name	Beginning of Last Month Balance	Amount Budgeted For Last Month	Actual Amount Paid Last Month	Remaining Debt Balance
	$	$	$	$
	$	$	$	$
	$	$	$	$
	$	$	$	$
	$	$	$	$
	$	$	$	$
	$	$	$	$
	$	$	$	$
	$	$	$	$
	$	$	$	$
Debt Totals	$	$	$	$

Recap Questions

1. What did I overspend on unnecessarily this month?
   Why do I think that happened?

....
....
....

2. What adjustments do I need to make to my spending
   to set my future self up in a much better position?

....
....
....

3. What will I tell myself if I spend over my daily budget one day?
   What actions will I take the following day(s) to get back on track?

....
....
....

4. In what ways can I be more supportive and forgiving of
   myself on this journey? How am I being too hard on myself?

....
....
....

Month 9
Days
249 - 279

Monthly Budget Preparation

My main financial goal for the month:

This Month's Forecast: __Income__

Income Category	Forecasted Amount
Total Active Income	$
Total Passive Income	$
Any Other Income	$
This Month's Forecasted Income	$

This Month's Budget: __Fixed Expenses__

Fixed Expense Category	Budget
Rent/Mortgage	$
Bills	$
Car Payments	$
Insurance	$
Subscriptions	$
Other	$
This Month's Fixed Expense Budget	$

Debt Clearing Planner

Debt Name	Total Balance Remaining	Budget	Total Month's Remaining to Complete
	$	$	
	$	$	
	$	$	
	$	$	
	$	$	
	$	$	
	$	$	
	$	$	
	$	$	
	$	$	
This Month's Debt Budget			

$ ....   − $ ....   − $ ....

(This Month's
Forecasted Income)
             (This Month's
Fixed Expense Budget)
             (This Month's
Debt Budget)

= $ ....

1. Now, choose how to allocate this remaining balance based on your personalized goals.

(This Month's
Remaining Balance)

Note: These two fields' totals should add up to "This Month's Remaining Balance."

$ ....　　　　$ ....

(This Month's
Savings Goal)
           (This Month's Flexible
Expense Budget)

2. Next, take "This Month's Flexible Expense Budget" and break it down based on the following categories:

This Month's Budget: **Flexible Expenses**	
Flexible Expense Category	**This Month's Budget**
Groceries	$
Household Necessities	$
Self-Care/Wellness	$
Entertainment	$
Outside Food/Drink	$
Other Indulgences	$
Other Transportation	$
Other	$
This Month's Flexible Expense Budget	$

3. Lastly, we'll calculate the daily budget you need to adhere to in order to achieve your monthly budgeting goal:

$ ....   ÷   ....   = $ ....

(This Month's Flexible
Expense Budget)
           (Total Days In
Upcoming Month)
           (Base Daily Budget)

_____ , 20 ___

(Month) (Year)

(This is an optional tool you can use to help get a visual overview of your entire month)

Mon	Tue	Wed	Thu	Fri	Sat	Sun

$ .... + $ .... = $ ....
(Base Daily Budget)   (Yesterday's Leftover Balance)   (Today's Daily Budget)

Day 249		
Flexible Expense Name	**Category**	**Today's Daily Budget:** $ _____
		- $
		- $
		- $
		- $
		- $
		- $
		- $
		- $
	Leftover Balance	**= $**

$ .... + $ .... = $ ....
(Base Daily Budget)   (Yesterday's Leftover Balance)   (Today's Daily Budget)

Day 250		
Flexible Expense Name	**Category**	**Today's Daily Budget:** $ _____
		- $
		- $
		- $
		- $
		- $
		- $
		- $
		- $
	Leftover Balance	**= $**

$ .... + $ .... = $ ....
(Base Daily Budget)   (Yesterday's Leftover Balance)   (Today's Daily Budget)

Day 251		
Flexible Expense Name	**Category**	**Today's Daily Budget:** $ _____
		– $
		– $
		– $
		– $
		– $
		– $
		– $
		– $
	Leftover Balance	**= $**

$ .... + $ .... = $ ....
(Base Daily Budget)   (Yesterday's Leftover Balance)   (Today's Daily Budget)

Day 252		
Flexible Expense Name	**Category**	**Today's Daily Budget:** $ _____
		– $
		– $
		– $
		– $
		– $
		– $
		– $
		– $
	Leftover Balance	**= $**

$ .... + $ .... = $ ....
(Base Daily Budget)   (Yesterday's Leftover Balance)   (Today's Daily Budget)

Day 253		
Flexible Expense Name	**Category**	**Today's Daily Budget:** $ _____
		- $
		- $
		- $
		- $
		- $
		- $
		- $
		- $
	Leftover Balance	**= $**

$ .... + $ .... = $ ....
(Base Daily Budget)   (Yesterday's Leftover Balance)   (Today's Daily Budget)

Day 254		
Flexible Expense Name	**Category**	**Today's Daily Budget:** $ _____
		- $
		- $
		- $
		- $
		- $
		- $
		- $
		- $
	Leftover Balance	**= $**

$ _____ + $ _____ = $ _____

(Base Daily Budget)   (Yesterday's Leftover Balance)   (Today's Daily Budget)

Day 255		
Flexible Expense Name	**Category**	**Today's Daily Budget:** $ _____
		- $
		- $
		- $
		- $
		- $
		- $
		- $
		- $
	Leftover Balance	= $

Weekly Reconciliation	
Flexible Expense Category	**This Week's Spend**
Groceries	$
Household Necessities	$
Self-Care/Wellness	$
Entertainment	$
Outside Food/Drink	$
Other Indulgences	$
Other Transportation	$
Other	$
Total Weekly Spend	$

$ .... + $ .... = $ ....
(Base Daily Budget)   (Yesterday's Leftover Balance)   (Today's Daily Budget)

Day 256		
Flexible Expense Name	**Category**	**Today's Daily Budget:** $ _____
		- $
		- $
		- $
		- $
		- $
		- $
		- $
		- $
	Leftover Balance	**= $**

$ .... + $ .... = $ ....
(Base Daily Budget)   (Yesterday's Leftover Balance)   (Today's Daily Budget)

Day 257		
Flexible Expense Name	**Category**	**Today's Daily Budget:** $ _____
		- $
		- $
		- $
		- $
		- $
		- $
		- $
		- $
	Leftover Balance	**= $**

$ .... + $ .... = $ ....
(Base Daily Budget)   (Yesterday's Leftover Balance)   (Today's Daily Budget)

Day 258		
Flexible Expense Name	**Category**	**Today's Daily Budget:** $ _____
		- $
		- $
		- $
		- $
		- $
		- $
		- $
	Leftover Balance	**= $**

$ .... + $ .... = $ ....
(Base Daily Budget)   (Yesterday's Leftover Balance)   (Today's Daily Budget)

Day 259		
Flexible Expense Name	**Category**	**Today's Daily Budget:** $ _____
		- $
		- $
		- $
		- $
		- $
		- $
		- $
		- $
	Leftover Balance	**= $**

$ .... + $ .... = $ ....
(Base Daily Budget)   (Yesterday's Leftover Balance)   (Today's Daily Budget)

Day 260		
Flexible Expense Name	**Category**	**Today's Daily Budget:** $ _____
		- $
		- $
		- $
		- $
		- $
		- $
		- $
		- $
	Leftover Balance	= $

$ .... + $ .... = $ ....
(Base Daily Budget)   (Yesterday's Leftover Balance)   (Today's Daily Budget)

Day 261		
Flexible Expense Name	**Category**	**Today's Daily Budget:** $ _____
		- $
		- $
		- $
		- $
		- $
		- $
		- $
		- $
	Leftover Balance	= $

$ .... (Base Daily Budget) + $ .... (Yesterday's Leftover Balance) = $ .... (Today's Daily Budget)

Day 262		
Flexible Expense Name	**Category**	**Today's Daily Budget:** $ _____
		- $
		- $
		- $
		- $
		- $
		- $
		- $
		- $
	Leftover Balance	= $

Weekly Reconciliation	
Flexible Expense Category	**This Week's Spend**
Groceries	$
Household Necessities	$
Self-Care/Wellness	$
Entertainment	$
Outside Food/Drink	$
Other Indulgences	$
Other Transportation	$
Other	$
Total Weekly Spend	$

$ ....
(Base Daily Budget)

+ $ ....
(Yesterday's Leftover Balance)

= $ ....
(Today's Daily Budget)

Day 263		
Flexible Expense Name	**Category**	**Today's Daily Budget:** $ _____
		- $
		- $
		- $
		- $
		- $
		- $
		- $
		- $
	Leftover Balance	= $

$ ....
(Base Daily Budget)

+ $ ....
(Yesterday's Leftover Balance)

= $ ....
(Today's Daily Budget)

Day 264		
Flexible Expense Name	**Category**	**Today's Daily Budget:** $ _____
		- $
		- $
		- $
		- $
		- $
		- $
		- $
		- $
	Leftover Balance	= $

$ .... + $ .... = $ ....
(Base Daily Budget)   (Yesterday's Leftover Balance)   (Today's Daily Budget)

Day 265		
Flexible Expense Name	**Category**	**Today's Daily Budget:** $ _____
		- $
		- $
		- $
		- $
		- $
		- $
		- $
		- $
	Leftover Balance	**= $**

$ .... + $ .... = $ ....
(Base Daily Budget)   (Yesterday's Leftover Balance)   (Today's Daily Budget)

Day 266		
Flexible Expense Name	**Category**	**Today's Daily Budget:** $ _____
		- $
		- $
		- $
		- $
		- $
		- $
		- $
		- $
	Leftover Balance	**= $**

$ .... + $ .... = $ ....
(Base Daily Budget)   (Yesterday's Leftover Balance)   (Today's Daily Budget)

Day 267		
Flexible Expense Name	**Category**	**Today's Daily Budget:** $\\$$ _____
		- $
		- $
		- $
		- $
		- $
		- $
		- $
		- $
	Leftover Balance	**= $**

$ .... + $ .... = $ ....
(Base Daily Budget)   (Yesterday's Leftover Balance)   (Today's Daily Budget)

Day 268		
Flexible Expense Name	**Category**	**Today's Daily Budget:** $\\$$ _____
		- $
		- $
		- $
		- $
		- $
		- $
		- $
		- $
	Leftover Balance	**= $**

$ .... + $ .... = $ ....

(Base Daily Budget)   (Yesterday's Leftover Balance)   (Today's Daily Budget)

Day 269		
Flexible Expense Name	**Category**	**Today's Daily Budget:** $ _____
		- $
		- $
		- $
		- $
		- $
		- $
		- $
		- $
	Leftover Balance	**= $**

Weekly Reconciliation	
Flexible Expense Category	**This Week's Spend**
Groceries	$
Household Necessities	$
Self-Care/Wellness	$
Entertainment	$
Outside Food/Drink	$
Other Indulgences	$
Other Transportation	$
Other	$
Total Weekly Spend	$

$ .... + $ .... = $ ....
(Base Daily Budget)   *(Yesterday's Leftover Balance)*   *(Today's Daily Budget)*

Day 270		
Flexible Expense Name	**Category**	**Today's Daily Budget:** $ _____
		- $
		- $
		- $
		- $
		- $
		- $
		- $
		- $
	Leftover Balance	**= $**

$ .... + $ .... = $ ....
(Base Daily Budget)   *(Yesterday's Leftover Balance)*   *(Today's Daily Budget)*

Day 271		
Flexible Expense Name	**Category**	**Today's Daily Budget:** $ _____
		- $
		- $
		- $
		- $
		- $
		- $
		- $
		- $
	Leftover Balance	**= $**

$ .... + $ .... = $ ....
(Base Daily Budget)   (Yesterday's Leftover Balance)   (Today's Daily Budget)

Day 272		
Flexible Expense Name	**Category**	**Today's Daily Budget:** $ _____
		- $
		- $
		- $
		- $
		- $
		- $
		- $
		- $
	Leftover Balance	= $

$ .... + $ .... = $ ....
(Base Daily Budget)   (Yesterday's Leftover Balance)   (Today's Daily Budget)

Day 273		
Flexible Expense Name	**Category**	**Today's Daily Budget:** $ _____
		- $
		- $
		- $
		- $
		- $
		- $
		- $
		- $
	Leftover Balance	= $

$ .... + $ .... = $ ....
(Base Daily Budget)   (Yesterday's Leftover Balance)   (Today's Daily Budget)

Day 274		
Flexible Expense Name	Category	Today's Daily Budget: $ _____
		- $
		- $
		- $
		- $
		- $
		- $
		- $
		- $
	Leftover Balance	= $

$ .... + $ .... = $ ....
(Base Daily Budget)   (Yesterday's Leftover Balance)   (Today's Daily Budget)

Day 275		
Flexible Expense Name	Category	Today's Daily Budget: $ _____
		- $
		- $
		- $
		- $
		- $
		- $
		- $
		- $
	Leftover Balance	= $

$ .... + $ .... = $ ....

(Base Daily Budget)   (Yesterday's Leftover Balance)   (Today's Daily Budget)

Day 276		
Flexible Expense Name	**Category**	**Today's Daily Budget:** $ _____
		- $
		- $
		- $
		- $
		- $
		- $
		- $
		- $
	Leftover Balance	**= $**

Weekly Reconciliation	
Flexible Expense Category	**This Week's Spend**
Groceries	$
Household Necessities	$
Self-Care/Wellness	$
Entertainment	$
Outside Food/Drink	$
Other Indulgences	$
Other Transportation	$
Other	$
Total Weekly Spend	$

$ .... + $ .... = $ ....
(Base Daily Budget)   (Yesterday's Leftover Balance)   (Today's Daily Budget)

Day 277		
Flexible Expense Name	Category	Today's Daily Budget: $ _____
		- $
		- $
		- $
		- $
		- $
		- $
		- $
		- $
	Leftover Balance	= $

$ .... + $ .... = $ ....
(Base Daily Budget)   (Yesterday's Leftover Balance)   (Today's Daily Budget)

Day 278		
Flexible Expense Name	Category	Today's Daily Budget: $ _____
		- $
		- $
		- $
		- $
		- $
		- $
		- $
		- $
	Leftover Balance	= $

$ .... + $ .... = $ ....
(Base Daily Budget)   (Yesterday's Leftover Balance)   (Today's Daily Budget)

Day 279		
Flexible Expense Name	**Category**	**Today's Daily Budget:** $ _____
		- $
		- $
		- $
		- $
		- $
		- $
		- $
		- $
	Leftover Balance	**= $**

Weekly Reconciliation	
Flexible Expense Category	**This Week's Spend**
Groceries	$
Household Necessities	$
Self-Care/Wellness	$
Entertainment	$
Outside Food/Drink	$
Other Indulgences	$
Other Transportation	$
Other	$
Total Weekly Spend	$

Month 9
Done.

Recapping Last Month

	Monthly Reconciliation: <u>**Income**</u>	
Income Category	**Last Month's Forecasted Income**	**Last Month's Actual Income**
Total Active Income	$	$
Total Passive Income	$	$
Any Other Income	$	$
Total Monthly Income	$	$

(You can easily get your "Actual Amount Spent Last Month" values by summing up the "Total Weekly Spend" values in your weekly reconciliations)

	Monthly Reconciliation: <u>**Flexible Expenses**</u>	
Flexible Expense Category	**Last Month's Budget**	**Actual Amount Spent Last Month**
Groceries	$	$
Household Necessities	$	$
Self-Care/Wellness	$	$
Entertainment	$	$
Outside Food/Drink	$	$
Other Indulgences	$	$
Other Transportation	$	$
Other	$	$
Total Monthly Flexible Expenses	$	$

Monthly Reconciliation: **Fixed Expenses**

Fixed Expense Category	Last Month's Budget	Actual Amount Spent Last Month
Rent/Mortgage	$	$
Bills	$	$
Car Payments	$	$
Insurance	$	$
Subscriptions	$	$
Other	$	$
Total Monthly Fixed Expenses	$	$

Monthly Reconciliation: **Debt Balance**

Debt Name	Beginning of Last Month Balance	Amount Budgeted For Last Month	Actual Amount Paid Last Month	Remaining Debt Balance
	$	$	$	$
	$	$	$	$
	$	$	$	$
	$	$	$	$
	$	$	$	$
	$	$	$	$
	$	$	$	$
	$	$	$	$
	$	$	$	$
	$	$	$	$
Debt Totals	$	$	$	$

Recap Questions

1. What did I overspend on unnecessarily this month?
   Why do I think that happened?

   ....

   ....

   ....

2. What adjustments do I need to make to my spending
   to set my future self up in a much better position?

   ....

   ....

   ....

3. What will I tell myself if I spend over my daily budget one day?
   What actions will I take the following day(s) to get back on track?

   ....

   ....

   ....

4. In what ways can I be more supportive and forgiving of
   myself on this journey? How am I being too hard on myself?

   ....

   ....

   ....

Month 10
Days
280 - 310

Monthly Budget Preparation

My main financial goal for the month:

This Month's Forecast: __Income__

Income Category	Forecasted Amount
Total Active Income	$
Total Passive Income	$
Any Other Income	$
This Month's Forecasted Income	$

This Month's Budget: __Fixed Expenses__

Fixed Expense Category	Budget
Rent/Mortgage	$
Bills	$
Car Payments	$
Insurance	$
Subscriptions	$
Other	$
This Month's Fixed Expense Budget	$

Debt Clearing Planner

Debt Name	Total Balance Remaining	Budget	Total Month's Remaining to Complete
	$	$	
	$	$	
	$	$	
	$	$	
	$	$	
	$	$	
	$	$	
	$	$	
	$	$	
	$	$	
This Month's Debt Budget			

$ _____ - $ _____ - $ _____

(This Month's
Forecasted Income)

(This Month's
Fixed Expense Budget)

(This Month's
Debt Budget)

= $ _____

(This Month's
Remaining Balance)

1. Now, choose how to allocate this remaining balance based on your personalized goals.

Note: These two fields' totals should add up to "This Month's Remaining Balance."

$ _____

(This Month's
Savings Goal)

$ _____

(This Month's Flexible
Expense Budget)

2. Next, take "This Month's Flexible Expense Budget" and break it down based on the following categories:

This Month's Budget: **Flexible Expenses**	
Flexible Expense Category	**This Month's Budget**
Groceries	$
Household Necessities	$
Self-Care/Wellness	$
Entertainment	$
Outside Food/Drink	$
Other Indulgences	$
Other Transportation	$
Other	$
This Month's Flexible Expense Budget	$

3. Lastly, we'll calculate the daily budget you need to adhere to in order to achieve your monthly budgeting goal:

$ _____ ÷ _____ = $ _____

(This Month's Flexible
Expense Budget)

(Total Days In
Upcoming Month)

(Base Daily Budget)

_____ , 20 _____

(Month)

(Year)

(This is an optional tool you can use to help get a visual overview of your entire month)

Mon	Tue	Wed	Thu	Fri	Sat	Sun

$ .... + $ .... = $ ....

(Base Daily Budget)   (Yesterday's Leftover Balance)   (Today's Daily Budget)

Day 280		
Flexible Expense Name	**Category**	**Today's Daily Budget:** **$** _____
		– $
		– $
		– $
		– $
		– $
		– $
		– $
		– $
	Leftover Balance	**= $**

$ .... + $ .... = $ ....

(Base Daily Budget)   (Yesterday's Leftover Balance)   (Today's Daily Budget)

Day 281		
Flexible Expense Name	**Category**	**Today's Daily Budget:** **$** _____
		– $
		– $
		– $
		– $
		– $
		– $
		– $
		– $
	Leftover Balance	**= $**

$ .... + $ .... = $ ....
(Base Daily Budget)   (Yesterday's Leftover Balance)   (Today's Daily Budget)

Day 282		
Flexible Expense Name	**Category**	**Today's Daily Budget:** $ _____
		- $
		- $
		- $
		- $
		- $
		- $
		- $
		- $
	Leftover Balance	= $

$ .... + $ .... = $ ....
(Base Daily Budget)   (Yesterday's Leftover Balance)   (Today's Daily Budget)

Day 283		
Flexible Expense Name	**Category**	**Today's Daily Budget:** $ _____
		- $
		- $
		- $
		- $
		- $
		- $
		- $
		- $
	Leftover Balance	= $

$ .... $\quad + \quad$ $ .... $\quad = \quad$ $ ....

(Base Daily Budget) (Yesterday's Leftover Balance) (Today's Daily Budget)

Day 284		
Flexible Expense Name	**Category**	**Today's Daily Budget:** $ _____
		- $
		- $
		- $
		- $
		- $
		- $
		- $
		- $
	Leftover Balance	**= $**

$ .... $\quad + \quad$ $ .... $\quad = \quad$ $ ....

(Base Daily Budget) (Yesterday's Leftover Balance) (Today's Daily Budget)

Day 285		
Flexible Expense Name	**Category**	**Today's Daily Budget:** $ _____
		- $
		- $
		- $
		- $
		- $
		- $
		- $
		- $
	Leftover Balance	**= $**

$ .... + $ .... = $ ....

(Base Daily Budget)   (Yesterday's Leftover Balance)   (Today's Daily Budget)

Day 286		
Flexible Expense Name	**Category**	**Today's Daily Budget:** $ _____
		- $
		- $
		- $
		- $
		- $
		- $
		- $
		- $
	Leftover Balance	**= $**

Weekly Reconciliation	
Flexible Expense Category	**This Week's Spend**
Groceries	$
Household Necessities	$
Self-Care/Wellness	$
Entertainment	$
Outside Food/Drink	$
Other Indulgences	$
Other Transportation	$
Other	$
Total Weekly Spend	$

$ .... + $ .... = $ ....
(Base Daily Budget)   (Yesterday's Leftover Balance)   (Today's Daily Budget)

Day 287		
Flexible Expense Name	**Category**	**Today's Daily Budget:** $ _____
		- $
		- $
		- $
		- $
		- $
		- $
		- $
		- $
	Leftover Balance	**= $**

$ .... + $ .... = $ ....
(Base Daily Budget)   (Yesterday's Leftover Balance)   (Today's Daily Budget)

Day 288		
Flexible Expense Name	**Category**	**Today's Daily Budget:** $ _____
		- $
		- $
		- $
		- $
		- $
		- $
		- $
		- $
	Leftover Balance	**= $**

$ _____ + $ _____ = $ _____
(Base Daily Budget)   *(Yesterday's Leftover Balance)*   *(Today's Daily Budget)*

Day 289		
Flexible Expense Name	**Category**	**Today's Daily Budget:** $ _____
		- $
		- $
		- $
		- $
		- $
		- $
		- $
		- $
	Leftover Balance	= $

$ _____ + $ _____ = $ _____
(Base Daily Budget)   *(Yesterday's Leftover Balance)*   *(Today's Daily Budget)*

Day 290		
Flexible Expense Name	**Category**	**Today's Daily Budget:** $ _____
		- $
		- $
		- $
		- $
		- $
		- $
		- $
		- $
	Leftover Balance	= $

$ .... + $ .... = $ ....
(Base Daily Budget)   (Yesterday's Leftover Balance)   (Today's Daily Budget)

Day 291		
Flexible Expense Name	**Category**	**Today's Daily Budget:** $ _____
		- $
		- $
		- $
		- $
		- $
		- $
		- $
		- $
	Leftover Balance	**= $**

$ .... + $ .... = $ ....
(Base Daily Budget)   (Yesterday's Leftover Balance)   (Today's Daily Budget)

Day 292		
Flexible Expense Name	**Category**	**Today's Daily Budget:** $ _____
		- $
		- $
		- $
		- $
		- $
		- $
		- $
		- $
	Leftover Balance	**= $**

$ .... + $ .... = $ ....
(Base Daily Budget)   (Yesterday's Leftover Balance)   (Today's Daily Budget)

Day 293		
Flexible Expense Name	**Category**	**Today's Daily Budget:** $ _____
		- $
		- $
		- $
		- $
		- $
		- $
		- $
		- $
	Leftover Balance	**= $**

Weekly Reconciliation	
Flexible Expense Category	**This Week's Spend**
Groceries	$
Household Necessities	$
Self-Care/Wellness	$
Entertainment	$
Outside Food/Drink	$
Other Indulgences	$
Other Transportation	$
Other	$
Total Weekly Spend	$

$ .... + $ .... = $ ....
(Base Daily Budget)   (Yesterday's Leftover Balance)   (Today's Daily Budget)

Day 294		
Flexible Expense Name	**Category**	**Today's Daily Budget:** $ _____
		- $
		- $
		- $
		- $
		- $
		- $
		- $
		- $
	Leftover Balance	= $

$ .... + $ .... = $ ....
(Base Daily Budget)   (Yesterday's Leftover Balance)   (Today's Daily Budget)

Day 295		
Flexible Expense Name	**Category**	**Today's Daily Budget:** $ _____
		- $
		- $
		- $
		- $
		- $
		- $
		- $
		- $
	Leftover Balance	= $

$ _____ + $ _____ = $ _____
(Base Daily Budget)   (Yesterday's Leftover Balance)   (Today's Daily Budget)

Day 296		
Flexible Expense Name	**Category**	**Today's Daily Budget:** $ _____
		- $
		- $
		- $
		- $
		- $
		- $
		- $
	Leftover Balance	= $

$ _____ + $ _____ = $ _____
(Base Daily Budget)   (Yesterday's Leftover Balance)   (Today's Daily Budget)

Day 297		
Flexible Expense Name	**Category**	**Today's Daily Budget:** $ _____
		- $
		- $
		- $
		- $
		- $
		- $
		- $
		- $
	Leftover Balance	= $

$ .... + $ .... = $ ....
(Base Daily Budget)   (Yesterday's Leftover Balance)   (Today's Daily Budget)

Day 298		
Flexible Expense Name	**Category**	**Today's Daily Budget:** $ _____
		- $
		- $
		- $
		- $
		- $
		- $
		- $
		- $
	Leftover Balance	**= $**

$ .... + $ .... = $ ....
(Base Daily Budget)   (Yesterday's Leftover Balance)   (Today's Daily Budget)

Day 299		
Flexible Expense Name	**Category**	**Today's Daily Budget:** $ _____
		- $
		- $
		- $
		- $
		- $
		- $
		- $
		- $
	Leftover Balance	**= $**

$ .... (Base Daily Budget) + $ .... (Yesterday's Leftover Balance) = $ .... (Today's Daily Budget)

Day 300		
Flexible Expense Name	**Category**	**Today's Daily Budget:** $ _____
		- $
		- $
		- $
		- $
		- $
		- $
		- $
		- $
	Leftover Balance	**= $**

Weekly Reconciliation	
Flexible Expense Category	**This Week's Spend**
Groceries	$
Household Necessities	$
Self-Care/Wellness	$
Entertainment	$
Outside Food/Drink	$
Other Indulgences	$
Other Transportation	$
Other	$
Total Weekly Spend	$

$ .... + $ .... = $ ....
(Base Daily Budget)   (Yesterday's Leftover Balance)   (Today's Daily Budget)

Day 301		
Flexible Expense Name	**Category**	**Today's Daily Budget:** $ _____
		- $
		- $
		- $
		- $
		- $
		- $
		- $
	Leftover Balance	**= $**

$ .... + $ .... = $ ....
(Base Daily Budget)   (Yesterday's Leftover Balance)   (Today's Daily Budget)

Day 302		
Flexible Expense Name	**Category**	**Today's Daily Budget:** $ _____
		- $
		- $
		- $
		- $
		- $
		- $
		- $
		- $
	Leftover Balance	**= $**

$ .... + $ .... = $ ....

(Base Daily Budget)   (Yesterday's Leftover Balance)   (Today's Daily Budget)

Day 303		
Flexible Expense Name	**Category**	**Today's Daily Budget:** $ _____
		- $
		- $
		- $
		- $
		- $
		- $
		- $
		- $
	Leftover Balance	**= $**

$ .... + $ .... = $ ....

(Base Daily Budget)   (Yesterday's Leftover Balance)   (Today's Daily Budget)

Day 304		
Flexible Expense Name	**Category**	**Today's Daily Budget:** $ _____
		- $
		- $
		- $
		- $
		- $
		- $
		- $
		- $
	Leftover Balance	**= $**

$ .... + $ .... = $ ....
(Base Daily Budget)   *(Yesterday's Leftover Balance)*   *(Today's Daily Budget)*

Day 305		
Flexible Expense Name	**Category**	**Today's Daily Budget:** $ _____
		- $
		- $
		- $
		- $
		- $
		- $
		- $
		- $
	Leftover Balance	= $

$ .... + $ .... = $ ....
(Base Daily Budget)   *(Yesterday's Leftover Balance)*   *(Today's Daily Budget)*

Day 306		
Flexible Expense Name	**Category**	**Today's Daily Budget:** $ _____
		- $
		- $
		- $
		- $
		- $
		- $
		- $
		- $
	Leftover Balance	= $

$ .... (Base Daily Budget) + $ .... (Yesterday's Leftover Balance) = $ .... (Today's Daily Budget)

Day 307		
Flexible Expense Name	**Category**	**Today's Daily Budget:** $ _____
		- $
		- $
		- $
		- $
		- $
		- $
		- $
		- $
	Leftover Balance	**= $**

Weekly Reconciliation	
Flexible Expense Category	**This Week's Spend**
Groceries	$
Household Necessities	$
Self-Care/Wellness	$
Entertainment	$
Outside Food/Drink	$
Other Indulgences	$
Other Transportation	$
Other	$
Total Weekly Spend	$

$ .... + $ .... = $ ....
(Base Daily Budget)   (Yesterday's Leftover Balance)   (Today's Daily Budget)

Day 308		
Flexible Expense Name	**Category**	**Today's Daily Budget:** $ _____
		- $
		- $
		- $
		- $
		- $
		- $
		- $
		- $
	Leftover Balance	**= $**

$ .... + $ .... = $ ....
(Base Daily Budget)   (Yesterday's Leftover Balance)   (Today's Daily Budget)

Day 309		
Flexible Expense Name	**Category**	**Today's Daily Budget:** $ _____
		- $
		- $
		- $
		- $
		- $
		- $
		- $
		- $
	Leftover Balance	**= $**

$ .... + $ .... = $ ....
(Base Daily Budget)   (Yesterday's Leftover Balance)   (Today's Daily Budget)

Day 310		
Flexible Expense Name	**Category**	**Today's Daily Budget:** $ _____
		- $
		- $
		- $
		- $
		- $
		- $
		- $
		- $
	Leftover Balance	**= $**

Weekly Reconciliation	
Flexible Expense Category	**This Week's Spend**
Groceries	$
Household Necessities	$
Self-Care/Wellness	$
Entertainment	$
Outside Food/Drink	$
Other Indulgences	$
Other Transportation	$
Other	$
Total Weekly Spend	$

Month 10

Done.

Recapping Last Month

	Monthly Reconciliation: <u>**Income**</u>	
Income Category	**Last Month's Forecasted Income**	**Last Month's Actual Income**
Total Active Income	$	$
Total Passive Income	$	$
Any Other Income	$	$
Total Monthly Income	$	$

(You can easily get your "Actual Amount Spent Last Month" values by summing up the "Total Weekly Spend" values in your weekly reconciliations)

	Monthly Reconciliation: <u>**Flexible Expenses**</u>	
Flexible Expense Category	**Last Month's Budget**	**Actual Amount Spent Last Month**
Groceries	$	$
Household Necessities	$	$
Self-Care/Wellness	$	$
Entertainment	$	$
Outside Food/Drink	$	$
Other Indulgences	$	$
Other Transportation	$	$
Other	$	$
Total Monthly Flexible Expenses	$	$

Monthly Reconciliation: **Fixed Expenses**

Fixed Expense Category	Last Month's Budget	Actual Amount Spent Last Month
Rent/Mortgage	$	$
Bills	$	$
Car Payments	$	$
Insurance	$	$
Subscriptions	$	$
Other	$	$
Total Monthly Fixed Expenses	$	$

Monthly Reconciliation: **Debt Balance**

Debt Name	Beginning of Last Month Balance	Amount Budgeted For Last Month	Actual Amount Paid Last Month	Remaining Debt Balance
	$	$	$	$
	$	$	$	$
	$	$	$	$
	$	$	$	$
	$	$	$	$
	$	$	$	$
	$	$	$	$
	$	$	$	$
	$	$	$	$
	$	$	$	$
Debt Totals	$	$	$	$

Recap Questions

1. What did I overspend on unnecessarily this month? Why do I think that happened?

....

....

....

2. What adjustments do I need to make to my spending to set my future self up in a much better position?

....

....

....

3. What will I tell myself if I spend over my daily budget one day? What actions will I take the following day(s) to get back on track?

....

....

....

4. In what ways can I be more supportive and forgiving of myself on this journey? How am I being too hard on myself?

....

....

....

Month 11
Days
311 - 341

Monthly Budget Preparation

My main financial goal for the month:

This Month's Forecast: __Income__

Income Category	Forecasted Amount
Total Active Income	$
Total Passive Income	$
Any Other Income	$
This Month's Forecasted Income	$

This Month's Budget: __Fixed Expenses__

Fixed Expense Category	Budget
Rent/Mortgage	$
Bills	$
Car Payments	$
Insurance	$
Subscriptions	$
Other	$
This Month's Fixed Expense Budget	$

Debt Clearing Planner

Debt Name	Total Balance Remaining	Budget	Total Month's Remaining to Complete
	$	$	
	$	$	
	$	$	
	$	$	
	$	$	
	$	$	
	$	$	
	$	$	
	$	$	
	$	$	
This Month's Debt Budget			

$ _____   – $ _____   – $ _____

(This Month's   (This Month's   (This Month's
Forecasted Income)   Fixed Expense Budget)   Debt Budget)

= $ _____

(This Month's
Remaining Balance)

1. Now, choose how to allocate this remaining balance based on your personalized goals.

Note: These two fields' totals should add up to "This Month's Remaining Balance."

$ _____ $ _____

(This Month's   (This Month's Flexible
Savings Goal)   Expense Budget)

2. Next, take "This Month's Flexible Expense Budget" and break it down based on the following categories:

This Month's Budget: **Flexible Expenses**	
Flexible Expense Category	**This Month's Budget**
Groceries	$
Household Necessities	$
Self-Care/Wellness	$
Entertainment	$
Outside Food/Drink	$
Other Indulgences	$
Other Transportation	$
Other	$
This Month's Flexible Expense Budget	$

3. Lastly, we'll calculate the daily budget you need to adhere to in order to achieve your monthly budgeting goal:

$ _____   ÷   _____   = $ _____

(This Month's Flexible   (Total Days In   (Base Daily Budget)
Expense Budget)   Upcoming Month)

_____, 20 ___

(This is an optional tool you can use to help
get a visual overview of your entire month)

Mon	Tue	Wed	Thu	Fri	Sat	Sun

$ .... + $ .... = $ ....

(Base Daily Budget)   (Yesterday's Leftover Balance)   (Today's Daily Budget)

Day 311		
Flexible Expense Name	**Category**	**Today's Daily Budget:** $ _____
		– $
		– $
		– $
		– $
		– $
		– $
		– $
		– $
	Leftover Balance	**= $**

$ .... + $ .... = $ ....

(Base Daily Budget)   (Yesterday's Leftover Balance)   (Today's Daily Budget)

Day 312		
Flexible Expense Name	**Category**	**Today's Daily Budget:** $ _____
		– $
		– $
		– $
		– $
		– $
		– $
		– $
		– $
	Leftover Balance	**= $**

$ .... + $ .... = $ ....
(Base Daily Budget)   (Yesterday's Leftover Balance)   (Today's Daily Budget)

Day 313		
Flexible Expense Name	**Category**	**Today's Daily Budget:** $ _____
		- $
		- $
		- $
		- $
		- $
		- $
		- $
		- $
	Leftover Balance	= $

$ .... + $ .... = $ ....

(Base Daily Budget)   (Yesterday's Leftover Balance)   (Today's Daily Budget)

Day 314		
Flexible Expense Name	**Category**	**Today's Daily Budget:** $ _____
		- $
		- $
		- $
		- $
		- $
		- $
		- $
		- $
	Leftover Balance	= $

$ .... + $ .... = $ ....
(Base Daily Budget)   (Yesterday's Leftover Balance)   (Today's Daily Budget)

Day 315		
Flexible Expense Name	**Category**	**Today's Daily Budget:** $ _____
		- $
		- $
		- $
		- $
		- $
		- $
		- $
		- $
	Leftover Balance	**= $**

$ .... + $ .... = $ ....
(Base Daily Budget)   (Yesterday's Leftover Balance)   (Today's Daily Budget)

Day 316		
Flexible Expense Name	**Category**	**Today's Daily Budget:** $ _____
		- $
		- $
		- $
		- $
		- $
		- $
		- $
		- $
	Leftover Balance	**= $**

$ .... + $ .... = $ ....

(Base Daily Budget)   (Yesterday's Leftover Balance)   (Today's Daily Budget)

Day 317		
Flexible Expense Name	**Category**	**Today's Daily Budget:** $ _____
		- $
		- $
		- $
		- $
		- $
		- $
		- $
		- $
	Leftover Balance	= $

Weekly Reconciliation	
Flexible Expense Category	**This Week's Spend**
Groceries	$
Household Necessities	$
Self-Care/Wellness	$
Entertainment	$
Outside Food/Drink	$
Other Indulgences	$
Other Transportation	$
Other	$
Total Weekly Spend	$

$ ....   + $ ....   = $ ....

(Base Daily Budget)   (Yesterday's Leftover Balance)   (Today's Daily Budget)

Day 318		
Flexible Expense Name	**Category**	**Today's Daily Budget:** **$** _____
		- $
		- $
		- $
		- $
		- $
		- $
		- $
		- $
	Leftover Balance	**= $**

$ ....   + $ ....   = $ ....

(Base Daily Budget)   (Yesterday's Leftover Balance)   (Today's Daily Budget)

Day 319		
Flexible Expense Name	**Category**	**Today's Daily Budget:** **$** _____
		- $
		- $
		- $
		- $
		- $
		- $
		- $
		- $
	Leftover Balance	**= $**

$ .... + $ .... = $ ....
(Base Daily Budget)   (Yesterday's Leftover Balance)   (Today's Daily Budget)

Day 320		
Flexible Expense Name	**Category**	**Today's Daily Budget:** $\$$ _____
		- $
		- $
		- $
		- $
		- $
		- $
		- $
		- $
	Leftover Balance	= $

$ .... + $ .... = $ ....
(Base Daily Budget)   (Yesterday's Leftover Balance)   (Today's Daily Budget)

Day 321		
Flexible Expense Name	**Category**	**Today's Daily Budget:** $\$$ _____
		- $
		- $
		- $
		- $
		- $
		- $
		- $
		- $
	Leftover Balance	= $

$ .... + $ .... = $ ....
(Base Daily Budget)   (Yesterday's Leftover Balance)   (Today's Daily Budget)

Day 322		
Flexible Expense Name	**Category**	**Today's Daily Budget:** $ _____
		- $
		- $
		- $
		- $
		- $
		- $
		- $
		- $
	Leftover Balance	= $

$ .... + $ .... = $ ....
(Base Daily Budget)   (Yesterday's Leftover Balance)   (Today's Daily Budget)

Day 323		
Flexible Expense Name	**Category**	**Today's Daily Budget:** $ _____
		- $
		- $
		- $
		- $
		- $
		- $
		- $
		- $
	Leftover Balance	= $

$ .... + $ .... = $ ....

(Base Daily Budget)   (Yesterday's Leftover Balance)   (Today's Daily Budget)

Day 324		
Flexible Expense Name	**Category**	**Today's Daily Budget:** $ _____
		– $
		– $
		– $
		– $
		– $
		– $
		– $
		– $
	Leftover Balance	= $

Weekly Reconciliation	
Flexible Expense Category	**This Week's Spend**
Groceries	$
Household Necessities	$
Self-Care/Wellness	$
Entertainment	$
Outside Food/Drink	$
Other Indulgences	$
Other Transportation	$
Other	$
Total Weekly Spend	$

$ .... + $ .... = $ ....
(Base Daily Budget)   (Yesterday's Leftover Balance)   (Today's Daily Budget)

Day 325		
Flexible Expense Name	**Category**	**Today's Daily Budget:** $ _____
		- $
		- $
		- $
		- $
		- $
		- $
		- $
		- $
	Leftover Balance	= $

$ .... + $ .... = $ ....
(Base Daily Budget)   (Yesterday's Leftover Balance)   (Today's Daily Budget)

Day 326		
Flexible Expense Name	**Category**	**Today's Daily Budget:** $ _____
		- $
		- $
		- $
		- $
		- $
		- $
		- $
		- $
	Leftover Balance	= $

$ .... + $ .... = $ ....
(Base Daily Budget)   (Yesterday's Leftover Balance)   (Today's Daily Budget)

Day 327		
Flexible Expense Name	**Category**	**Today's Daily Budget:** $ _____
		- $
		- $
		- $
		- $
		- $
		- $
		- $
		- $
	Leftover Balance	= $

$ .... + $ .... = $ ....
(Base Daily Budget)   (Yesterday's Leftover Balance)   (Today's Daily Budget)

Day 328		
Flexible Expense Name	**Category**	**Today's Daily Budget:** $ _____
		- $
		- $
		- $
		- $
		- $
		- $
		- $
		- $
	Leftover Balance	= $

$ .... + $ .... = $ ....
(Base Daily Budget)   (Yesterday's Leftover Balance)   (Today's Daily Budget)

Day 329		
Flexible Expense Name	**Category**	**Today's Daily Budget:** $ _____
		- $
		- $
		- $
		- $
		- $
		- $
		- $
		- $
	Leftover Balance	= $

$ .... + $ .... = $ ....
(Base Daily Budget)   (Yesterday's Leftover Balance)   (Today's Daily Budget)

Day 330		
Flexible Expense Name	**Category**	**Today's Daily Budget:** $ _____
		- $
		- $
		- $
		- $
		- $
		- $
		- $
		- $
	Leftover Balance	= $

$ .... + $ .... = $ ....
(Base Daily Budget)   (Yesterday's Leftover Balance)   (Today's Daily Budget)

Day 331		
Flexible Expense Name	**Category**	**Today's Daily Budget:** $ _____
		- $
		- $
		- $
		- $
		- $
		- $
		- $
		- $
	Leftover Balance	= $

Weekly Reconciliation	
Flexible Expense Category	**This Week's Spend**
Groceries	$
Household Necessities	$
Self-Care/Wellness	$
Entertainment	$
Outside Food/Drink	$
Other Indulgences	$
Other Transportation	$
Other	$
Total Weekly Spend	$

$ .... + $ .... = $ ....
(Base Daily Budget)   (Yesterday's Leftover Balance)   (Today's Daily Budget)

Day 332		
Flexible Expense Name	**Category**	**Today's Daily Budget:** $ _____
		– $
		– $
		– $
		– $
		– $
		– $
		– $
		– $
	Leftover Balance	= $

$ .... + $ .... = $ ....
(Base Daily Budget)   (Yesterday's Leftover Balance)   (Today's Daily Budget)

Day 333		
Flexible Expense Name	**Category**	**Today's Daily Budget:** $ _____
		– $
		– $
		– $
		– $
		– $
		– $
		– $
		– $
	Leftover Balance	= $

$ .... + $ .... = $ ....

(Base Daily Budget)   (Yesterday's Leftover Balance)   (Today's Daily Budget)

Day 334		
Flexible Expense Name	**Category**	**Today's Daily Budget:** $ _____
		- $
		- $
		- $
		- $
		- $
		- $
		- $
	Leftover Balance	= $

$ .... + $ .... = $ ....

(Base Daily Budget)   (Yesterday's Leftover Balance)   (Today's Daily Budget)

Day 335		
Flexible Expense Name	**Category**	**Today's Daily Budget:** $ _____
		- $
		- $
		- $
		- $
		- $
		- $
		- $
		- $
	Leftover Balance	= $

$ .... + $ .... = $ ....

(Base Daily Budget) (Yesterday's Leftover Balance) (Today's Daily Budget)

Day 336		
Flexible Expense Name	**Category**	**Today's Daily Budget:** $ _____
		- $
		- $
		- $
		- $
		- $
		- $
		- $
		- $
	Leftover Balance	**= $**

$ .... + $ .... = $ ....

(Base Daily Budget) (Yesterday's Leftover Balance) (Today's Daily Budget)

Day 337		
Flexible Expense Name	**Category**	**Today's Daily Budget:** $ _____
		- $
		- $
		- $
		- $
		- $
		- $
		- $
		- $
	Leftover Balance	**= $**

$ .... + $ .... = $ ....
(Base Daily Budget)   (Yesterday's Leftover Balance)   (Today's Daily Budget)

Day 338		
Flexible Expense Name	**Category**	**Today's Daily Budget:** $ _____
		- $
		- $
		- $
		- $
		- $
		- $
		- $
		- $
	Leftover Balance	**= $**

Weekly Reconciliation	
Flexible Expense Category	**This Week's Spend**
Groceries	$
Household Necessities	$
Self-Care/Wellness	$
Entertainment	$
Outside Food/Drink	$
Other Indulgences	$
Other Transportation	$
Other	$
Total Weekly Spend	$

$ .... + $ .... = $ ....
(Base Daily Budget)   (Yesterday's Leftover Balance)   (Today's Daily Budget)

Day 339		
Flexible Expense Name	**Category**	**Today's Daily Budget:** $ _____
		- $
		- $
		- $
		- $
		- $
		- $
		- $
		- $
	Leftover Balance	= $

$ .... + $ .... = $ ....
(Base Daily Budget)   (Yesterday's Leftover Balance)   (Today's Daily Budget)

Day 340		
Flexible Expense Name	**Category**	**Today's Daily Budget:** $ _____
		- $
		- $
		- $
		- $
		- $
		- $
		- $
		- $
	Leftover Balance	= $

$ .... + $ .... = $ ....
(Base Daily Budget)   (Yesterday's Leftover Balance)   (Today's Daily Budget)

Day 341		
Flexible Expense Name	**Category**	**Today's Daily Budget:** $ _____
		- $
		- $
		- $
		- $
		- $
		- $
		- $
		- $
	Leftover Balance	= $

Weekly Reconciliation	
Flexible Expense Category	**This Week's Spend**
Groceries	$
Household Necessities	$
Self-Care/Wellness	$
Entertainment	$
Outside Food/Drink	$
Other Indulgences	$
Other Transportation	$
Other	$
Total Weekly Spend	$

Month 11

Done.

Recapping Last Month

Monthly Reconciliation: **Income**		
Income Category	**Last Month's Forecasted Income**	**Last Month's Actual Income**
Total Active Income	$	$
Total Passive Income	$	$
Any Other Income	$	$
Total Monthly Income	$	$

(You can easily get your "Actual Amount Spent Last Month" values by summing up the "Total Weekly Spend" values in your weekly reconciliations)

Monthly Reconciliation: **Flexible Expenses**		
Flexible Expense Category	**Last Month's Budget**	**Actual Amount Spent Last Month**
Groceries	$	$
Household Necessities	$	$
Self-Care/Wellness	$	$
Entertainment	$	$
Outside Food/Drink	$	$
Other Indulgences	$	$
Other Transportation	$	$
Other	$	$
Total Monthly Flexible Expenses	$	$

Monthly Reconciliation: <u>Fixed Expenses</u>

Fixed Expense Category	Last Month's Budget	Actual Amount Spent Last Month
Rent/Mortgage	$	$
Bills	$	$
Car Payments	$	$
Insurance	$	$
Subscriptions	$	$
Other	$	$
Total Monthly Fixed Expenses	$	$

Monthly Reconciliation: <u>Debt Balance</u>

Debt Name	Beginning of Last Month Balance	Amount Budgeted For Last Month	Actual Amount Paid Last Month	Remaining Debt Balance
	$	$	$	$
	$	$	$	$
	$	$	$	$
	$	$	$	$
	$	$	$	$
	$	$	$	$
	$	$	$	$
	$	$	$	$
	$	$	$	$
	$	$	$	$
Debt Totals	$	$	$	$

Recap Questions

1. What did I overspend on unnecessarily this month?
   Why do I think that happened?

....

....

....

2. What adjustments do I need to make to my spending
   to set my future self up in a much better position?

....

....

....

3. What will I tell myself if I spend over my daily budget one day?
   What actions will I take the following day(s) to get back on track?

....

....

....

4. In what ways can I be more supportive and forgiving of
   myself on this journey? How am I being too hard on myself?

....

....

....

Month 12
Days
342 - 372

Monthly Budget Preparation

My main financial goal for the month:

This Month's Forecast: __Income__

Income Category	Forecasted Amount
Total Active Income	$
Total Passive Income	$
Any Other Income	$
This Month's Forecasted Income	$

This Month's Budget: __Fixed Expenses__

Fixed Expense Category	Budget
Rent/Mortgage	$
Bills	$
Car Payments	$
Insurance	$
Subscriptions	$
Other	$
This Month's Fixed Expense Budget	$

Debt Clearing Planner

Debt Name	Total Balance Remaining	Budget	Total Month's Remaining to Complete
	$	$	
	$	$	
	$	$	
	$	$	
	$	$	
	$	$	
	$	$	
	$	$	
	$	$	
	$	$	
This Month's Debt Budget			

$ _____ - $ _____ - $ _____

(This Month's
Forecasted Income)   (This Month's
Fixed Expense Budget)   (This Month's
Debt Budget)

= $ _____

(This Month's
Remaining Balance)

1. Now, choose how to allocate this remaining balance based on your personalized goals.

Note: These two fields' totals should add up to "This Month's Remaining Balance."

$ _____ $ _____

(This Month's
Savings Goal)   (This Month's Flexible
Expense Budget)

2. Next, take "This Month's Flexible Expense Budget" and break it down based on the following categories:

This Month's Budget: **Flexible Expenses**	
Flexible Expense Category	**This Month's Budget**
Groceries	$
Household Necessities	$
Self-Care/Wellness	$
Entertainment	$
Outside Food/Drink	$
Other Indulgences	$
Other Transportation	$
Other	$
This Month's Flexible Expense Budget	$

3. Lastly, we'll calculate the daily budget you need to adhere to in order to achieve your monthly budgeting goal:

$ _____   ÷   _____   = $ _____

(This Month's Flexible
Expense Budget)   (Total Days In
Upcoming Month)   (Base Daily Budget)

_____ , 20 _____

(Month)   (Year)

(This is an optional tool you can use to help get a visual overview of your entire month)

Mon	Tue	Wed	Thu	Fri	Sat	Sun

$ .... + $ .... = $ ....
(Base Daily Budget)   (Yesterday's Leftover Balance)   (Today's Daily Budget)

Day 342		
Flexible Expense Name	**Category**	**Today's Daily Budget:** $ _____
		- $
		- $
		- $
		- $
		- $
		- $
		- $
		- $
	Leftover Balance	**= $**

$ .... + $ .... = $ ....
(Base Daily Budget)   (Yesterday's Leftover Balance)   (Today's Daily Budget)

Day 343		
Flexible Expense Name	**Category**	**Today's Daily Budget:** $ _____
		- $
		- $
		- $
		- $
		- $
		- $
		- $
		- $
	Leftover Balance	**= $**

$ .... + $ .... = $ ....
(Base Daily Budget)   (Yesterday's Leftover Balance)   (Today's Daily Budget)

Day 344		
Flexible Expense Name	**Category**	**Today's Daily Budget:** $ _____
		- $
		- $
		- $
		- $
		- $
		- $
		- $
		- $
	Leftover Balance	= $

$ .... + $ .... = $ ....
(Base Daily Budget)   (Yesterday's Leftover Balance)   (Today's Daily Budget)

Day 345		
Flexible Expense Name	**Category**	**Today's Daily Budget:** $ _____
		- $
		- $
		- $
		- $
		- $
		- $
		- $
		- $
	Leftover Balance	= $

$ .... + $ .... = $ ....

(Base Daily Budget)   (Yesterday's Leftover Balance)   (Today's Daily Budget)

Day 346		
Flexible Expense Name	**Category**	**Today's Daily Budget:** $ _____
		- $
		- $
		- $
		- $
		- $
		- $
		- $
		- $
	Leftover Balance	**= $**

$ .... + $ .... = $ ....

(Base Daily Budget)   (Yesterday's Leftover Balance)   (Today's Daily Budget)

Day 347		
Flexible Expense Name	**Category**	**Today's Daily Budget:** $ _____
		- $
		- $
		- $
		- $
		- $
		- $
		- $
		- $
	Leftover Balance	**= $**

$ .... + $ .... = $ ....
(Base Daily Budget)   (Yesterday's Leftover Balance)   (Today's Daily Budget)

Day 348		
Flexible Expense Name	**Category**	**Today's Daily Budget:** $ _____
		- $
		- $
		- $
		- $
		- $
		- $
		- $
		- $
	Leftover Balance	**= $**

Weekly Reconciliation	
Flexible Expense Category	**This Week's Spend**
Groceries	$
Household Necessities	$
Self-Care/Wellness	$
Entertainment	$
Outside Food/Drink	$
Other Indulgences	$
Other Transportation	$
Other	$
Total Weekly Spend	$

$ .... + $ .... = $ ....
(Base Daily Budget)   (Yesterday's Leftover Balance)   (Today's Daily Budget)

Day 349		
Flexible Expense Name	**Category**	**Today's Daily Budget:** $ _____
		- $
		- $
		- $
		- $
		- $
		- $
		- $
		- $
	Leftover Balance	= $

$ .... + $ .... = $ ....
(Base Daily Budget)   (Yesterday's Leftover Balance)   (Today's Daily Budget)

Day 350		
Flexible Expense Name	**Category**	**Today's Daily Budget:** $ _____
		- $
		- $
		- $
		- $
		- $
		- $
		- $
		- $
	Leftover Balance	= $

$ .... + $ .... = $ ....
(Base Daily Budget)   (Yesterday's Leftover Balance)   (Today's Daily Budget)

Day 351		
Flexible Expense Name	**Category**	**Today's Daily Budget:** $ _____
		- $
		- $
		- $
		- $
		- $
		- $
		- $
		- $
	Leftover Balance	= $

$ .... + $ .... = $ ....
(Base Daily Budget)   (Yesterday's Leftover Balance)   (Today's Daily Budget)

Day 352		
Flexible Expense Name	**Category**	**Today's Daily Budget:** $ _____
		- $
		- $
		- $
		- $
		- $
		- $
		- $
		- $
	Leftover Balance	= $

$ ....   + $ ....   = $ ....

(Base Daily Budget)   (Yesterday's Leftover Balance)   (Today's Daily Budget)

Day 353		
Flexible Expense Name	**Category**	**Today's Daily Budget:** $ _____
		- $
		- $
		- $
		- $
		- $
		- $
		- $
		- $
	Leftover Balance	= $

$ ....   + $ ....   = $ ....

(Base Daily Budget)   (Yesterday's Leftover Balance)   (Today's Daily Budget)

Day 354		
Flexible Expense Name	**Category**	**Today's Daily Budget:** $ _____
		- $
		- $
		- $
		- $
		- $
		- $
		- $
		- $
	Leftover Balance	= $

$ .... + $ .... = $ ....
(Base Daily Budget)   (Yesterday's Leftover Balance)   (Today's Daily Budget)

Day 355		
Flexible Expense Name	**Category**	**Today's Daily Budget:** $ _____
		- $
		- $
		- $
		- $
		- $
		- $
		- $
		- $
	Leftover Balance	**= $**

Weekly Reconciliation	
Flexible Expense Category	**This Week's Spend**
Groceries	$
Household Necessities	$
Self-Care/Wellness	$
Entertainment	$
Outside Food/Drink	$
Other Indulgences	$
Other Transportation	$
Other	$
Total Weekly Spend	$

$ .... + $ .... = $ ....
(Base Daily Budget)   *(Yesterday's Leftover Balance)*   *(Today's Daily Budget)*

Day 356		
Flexible Expense Name	**Category**	**Today's Daily Budget:** $ _____
		- $
		- $
		- $
		- $
		- $
		- $
		- $
		- $
	Leftover Balance	**= $**

$ .... + $ .... = $ ....
(Base Daily Budget)   *(Yesterday's Leftover Balance)*   *(Today's Daily Budget)*

Day 357		
Flexible Expense Name	**Category**	**Today's Daily Budget:** $ _____
		- $
		- $
		- $
		- $
		- $
		- $
		- $
		- $
	Leftover Balance	**= $**

$ .... + $ .... = $ ....
(Base Daily Budget)   (Yesterday's Leftover Balance)   (Today's Daily Budget)

Day 358		
Flexible Expense Name	**Category**	**Today's Daily Budget:** $ _____
		- $
		- $
		- $
		- $
		- $
		- $
		- $
		- $
	Leftover Balance	**= $**

$ .... + $ .... = $ ....
(Base Daily Budget)   (Yesterday's Leftover Balance)   (Today's Daily Budget)

Day 359		
Flexible Expense Name	**Category**	**Today's Daily Budget:** $ _____
		- $
		- $
		- $
		- $
		- $
		- $
		- $
		- $
	Leftover Balance	**= $**

$ .... + $ .... = $ ....
(Base Daily Budget)   (Yesterday's Leftover Balance)   (Today's Daily Budget)

Day 360		
Flexible Expense Name	**Category**	**Today's Daily Budget:** $ _____
		- $
		- $
		- $
		- $
		- $
		- $
		- $
		- $
	Leftover Balance	= $

$ .... + $ .... = $ ....
(Base Daily Budget)   (Yesterday's Leftover Balance)   (Today's Daily Budget)

Day 361		
Flexible Expense Name	**Category**	**Today's Daily Budget:** $ _____
		- $
		- $
		- $
		- $
		- $
		- $
		- $
		- $
	Leftover Balance	= $

$ .... + $ .... = $ ....
(Base Daily Budget)   (Yesterday's Leftover Balance)   (Today's Daily Budget)

Day 362		
Flexible Expense Name	**Category**	**Today's Daily Budget:** $ _____
		- $
		- $
		- $
		- $
		- $
		- $
		- $
		- $
	Leftover Balance	**= $**

Weekly Reconciliation	
Flexible Expense Category	**This Week's Spend**
Groceries	$
Household Necessities	$
Self-Care/Wellness	$
Entertainment	$
Outside Food/Drink	$
Other Indulgences	$
Other Transportation	$
Other	$
Total Weekly Spend	$

$ .... + $ .... = $ ....

(Base Daily Budget)   (Yesterday's Leftover Balance)   (Today's Daily Budget)

Day 363		
Flexible Expense Name	**Category**	**Today's Daily Budget:** $ _____
		- $
		- $
		- $
		- $
		- $
		- $
		- $
	Leftover Balance	**= $**

$ .... + $ .... = $ ....

(Base Daily Budget)   (Yesterday's Leftover Balance)   (Today's Daily Budget)

Day 364		
Flexible Expense Name	**Category**	**Today's Daily Budget:** $ _____
		- $
		- $
		- $
		- $
		- $
		- $
		- $
		- $
	Leftover Balance	**= $**

$ .... + $ .... = $ ....
(Base Daily Budget)   (Yesterday's Leftover Balance)   (Today's Daily Budget)

Day 365		
Flexible Expense Name	**Category**	**Today's Daily Budget:** $ _____
		- $
		- $
		- $
		- $
		- $
		- $
		- $
		- $
	Leftover Balance	= $

$ .... + $ .... = $ ....
(Base Daily Budget)   (Yesterday's Leftover Balance)   (Today's Daily Budget)

Day 366		
Flexible Expense Name	**Category**	**Today's Daily Budget:** $ _____
		- $
		- $
		- $
		- $
		- $
		- $
		- $
		- $
	Leftover Balance	= $

$ ....   + $ ....   = $ ....

(Base Daily Budget)   *(Yesterday's Leftover Balance)*   *(Today's Daily Budget)*

Day 367		
Flexible Expense Name	**Category**	**Today's Daily Budget:** $ _____
		- $
		- $
		- $
		- $
		- $
		- $
		- $
		- $
	Leftover Balance	= $

$ ....   + $ ....   = $ ....

(Base Daily Budget)   *(Yesterday's Leftover Balance)*   *(Today's Daily Budget)*

Day 368		
Flexible Expense Name	**Category**	**Today's Daily Budget:** $ _____
		- $
		- $
		- $
		- $
		- $
		- $
		- $
		- $
	Leftover Balance	= $

$ _____ + $ _____ = $ _____
(Base Daily Budget)   (Yesterday's Leftover Balance)   (Today's Daily Budget)

Day 369		
Flexible Expense Name	**Category**	**Today's Daily Budget:** $ _____
		- $
		- $
		- $
		- $
		- $
		- $
		- $
		- $
	Leftover Balance	= $

Weekly Reconciliation	
Flexible Expense Category	**This Week's Spend**
Groceries	$
Household Necessities	$
Self-Care/Wellness	$
Entertainment	$
Outside Food/Drink	$
Other Indulgences	$
Other Transportation	$
Other	$
Total Weekly Spend	$

$ .... + $ .... = $ ....
  (Base Daily Budget)   (Yesterday's Leftover Balance)   (Today's Daily Budget)

Day 370		
Flexible Expense Name	**Category**	**Today's Daily Budget:** $ _____
		- $
		- $
		- $
		- $
		- $
		- $
		- $
		- $
	Leftover Balance	= $

$ .... + $ .... = $ ....
  (Base Daily Budget)   (Yesterday's Leftover Balance)   (Today's Daily Budget)

Day 371		
Flexible Expense Name	**Category**	**Today's Daily Budget:** $ _____
		- $
		- $
		- $
		- $
		- $
		- $
		- $
		- $
	Leftover Balance	= $

$ .... + $ .... = $ ....
(Base Daily Budget)   *(Yesterday's Leftover Balance)*   *(Today's Daily Budget)*

Day 372		
Flexible Expense Name	**Category**	**Today's Daily Budget:** $ _____
		- $
		- $
		- $
		- $
		- $
		- $
		- $
		- $
	Leftover Balance	**= $**

Weekly Reconciliation	
Flexible Expense Category	**This Week's Spend**
Groceries	$
Household Necessities	$
Self-Care/Wellness	$
Entertainment	$
Outside Food/Drink	$
Other Indulgences	$
Other Transportation	$
Other	$
Total Weekly Spend	$

Month 12

Done.

Congratulations!

You've mastered the Budgeting Mastery Journal!

Recapping Last Month

Monthly Reconciliation: **Income**		
Income Category	**Last Month's Forecasted Income**	**Last Month's Actual Income**
Total Active Income	$	$
Total Passive Income	$	$
Any Other Income	$	$
Total Monthly Income	$	$

(You can easily get your "Actual Amount Spent Last Month" values by summing up the "Total Weekly Spend" values in your weekly reconciliations)

Monthly Reconciliation: **Flexible Expenses**		
Flexible Expense Category	**Last Month's Budget**	**Actual Amount Spent Last Month**
Groceries	$	$
Household Necessities	$	$
Self-Care/Wellness	$	$
Entertainment	$	$
Outside Food/Drink	$	$
Other Indulgences	$	$
Other Transportation	$	$
Other	$	$
Total Monthly Flexible Expenses	$	$

Monthly Reconciliation: **Fixed Expenses**

Fixed Expense Category	Last Month's Budget	Actual Amount Spent Last Month
Rent/Mortgage	$	$
Bills	$	$
Car Payments	$	$
Insurance	$	$
Subscriptions	$	$
Other	$	$
Total Monthly Fixed Expenses	$	$

Monthly Reconciliation: **Debt Balance**

Debt Name	Beginning of Last Month Balance	Amount Budgeted For Last Month	Actual Amount Paid Last Month	Remaining Debt Balance
	$	$	$	$
	$	$	$	$
	$	$	$	$
	$	$	$	$
	$	$	$	$
	$	$	$	$
	$	$	$	$
	$	$	$	$
	$	$	$	$
	$	$	$	$
Debt Totals	$	$	$	$

Recap Questions

1. What did I overspend on unnecessarily this month?
   Why do I think that happened?

....

....

....

2. What adjustments do I need to make to my spending
   to set my future self up in a much better position?

....

....

....

3. What will I tell myself if I spend over my daily budget one day?
   What actions will I take the following day(s) to get back on track?

....

....

....

4. In what ways can I be more supportive and forgiving of
   myself on this journey? How am I being too hard on myself?

....

....

....

- Fin -

So... What Now?

Although you should feel very accomplished for getting through this entire journal... know that you built this habit to continually improve your life. Don't stop now. This is only the beginning.

One huge factor to this is tracking your progress. Once you stop tracking, it makes it exponentially easier for you to lose your momentum in practicing daily gratitude (due to the lack of accountability with yourself).

Remember: **Every month you're intentional about spending and saving will lead to increased financial peace.**

You only stand to gain from continuing this habit.

Meet the Habit Nest Cofounders

Amir Atighehchi

Amir graduated from USC's Marshall School of Business in 2013. He got his first taste of entrepreneurship during college with Mikey when they co-founded a bicycle lock company called Nutlock. It wasn't until after college when he opened his eyes to the world of personal development and healthy habits. Amir is fascinated by creative challenges and entrepreneurship.

Mikey Ahdoot

Mikey transformed his life from a 200+ pound video game addict to someone who was doing 17 daily habits consistently at one point. From ice cold showers to brainstorming 10 ideas a day (shoutout to James Altucher) to celebrating life every single day, he is first hand becoming a habit routine machine that sets himself up for success daily. He is a graduate of USC's Marshall School of Business and a proud Trojan.

Ari Banayan

Ari graduated from the University of Southern California Gould School of Law in 2016. Through his own life experience, he understands how important it is to take care of ourselves mentally, physically and emotionally to operate at maximum capacity. He uses waking up early, reading, meditation, exercise, and a healthy diet to create a solid foundation for his everyday life.

326

Read all of our full stories here:
habitnest.com/aboutus

Shop Habit Nest Products

Lifestyle Products

*All of our lifestyle journals come with **daily content** (including Pro-Tips, Daily Challenges, Practical Resources, & more) to inspire you and give you bite-sized information to use along your journey. They also contain **daily questions aimed at holding you accountable** to ingraining that habit into your life.*

- **The Morning Sidekick Journal Series**
  A set of guided morning planners that help you conquer your mornings and conquer your life. This complete 4-volume series covers 1-year of morning routines.

- **The Evening Routine & Sleep Sidekick Journal**
  Helps you to wind down your days peacefully, prepare for each next day, and get the most rejuvenating sleep of your life.

- **The Gratitude Sidekick Journal**
  A research-based journal that will help make an **attitude of appreciation** a core part of who you are.

- **The Meditation Sidekick Journal**
  Built to give you all the tools you need to stay consistent with a meditation practice.

- **The Nutrition Sidekick Journal**
  Your nutrition tracker, informational guide, and coach, all in one.

- **The Budgeting Sidekick Journal Series**
  The most simple-yet-effective budgeting guide in the world, helping you find full clarity on your budgeting goals and to achieve financial freedom. Set spending goals, track your daily spending, and reconcile along the way. Contains 2 volumes which cover well over a year of budgeting.

Fitness Products

Our no-nonsense fitness books have fully guided fitness routines.
No thinking required; just open the books and follow along.

- ### The Weightlifting Gym Buddy Journal Series
A set of guided personal training programs aimed at helping you have the best workouts of your life. This complete 4-volume series covers 1-year of weightlifting workouts.

- ### The Bodyweight / Dumbbell Home Workout Journals
Specifically focus on HOME workout programs that require minimal-to-no equipment to complete.

- ### The Badass Body Goals Journal
An at-home-friendly fitness journal that focuses on HIIT and circuit workouts. This journal comes with a full video guide you can play and follow along.

Other Products

- ### The Habit Nest Mobile Application
The app will offer a digital representation of our journals so you can stay on your Habit Nest journey while mobile. Available on iOS & Android.

- ### The Habit Nest Daily Planner
Plan your day including your top priorities, smaller 5-minute tasks, and all your to-dos. Get optional suggestions for ways to start your mornings and end your evenings with as well.

- ### George The Short-Necked Giraffe (Children's Book)
Follow along George's journey as he learns the hard way that fully accepting himself, exactly the way he is, is the only path to living his happiest life.

Shop all products here: **habitnest.com/store**

The Habit Nest Mobile App

When Habit Nest was initially founded, it was supposed to be in mobile app form from the start. We tried for a year as a team of three young founders with no outside funding to get a mobile app built, but we never could pull it off back then.

We switched to paper journals that worked using the same concept, which you're currently holding. Now, 5 years and hundreds of thousands of journals sold later, **we're finally in a place to chase our dream** of creating an app.

It's making us a bit emotional as things have come full circle and we're unbelievably **thankful for every single customer (like you)** who has helped us get here, shared their ups and downs with us, and really just **given us a chance** to grow our little company that sincerely cares.

We've been working extremely hard to be able to create the Habit Nest mobile app this year and **it will be live in the iOS and Android app stores in January 2021.**

The app will offer a **digital representation of our journals** so you can stay on your Habit Nest journey while mobile.

If you're interested in seeing how it can help you, feel free to see more at **habitnest.com/app**

Thank you for making this possible.

With hugs and a lot of love,
Mikey Ahdoot, Ari Banayan, & Amir Atighehchi
Cofounders of Habit Nest

Share The Love

If you're reading this, that means you've come pretty far from where you were when starting. You should be extremely proud of yourself!

If you believe this journal has had a positive impact on your life, we invite you to consider gifting a new one to a friend.

Is there a holiday coming up? Is there a special birthday around the corner? Or do you just want to put a smile on someone's face and do something incredible for them?

Gifting this journal is the absolute best way to show any gratitude you may have for what we've written here, as well as serving as a force of good through giving back to others. And you can rest assured that you're helping improve another person's life at the same time.

We created a discount code for getting this far that can be used for any Habit Nest journal (make sure to use the same email address you placed the order with).

If you decide to, feel free to re-order here:
habitnest.com/budgeting

Use code **budgetingchamp15** for **15% off!**